Contents

Foreword

The Highway Code might be seen by some as a motoring manual but, from its inception in 1931, it was meant for *all* road users, not just motorists. The first edition – all 18 pages of it, one of which was devoted to cycling – introduced the principle that cyclists and pedestrians were also responsible for road safety.

The first rule in *The Highway Code* of 1931 was 'Always be considerate towards others'. This concept didn't originate with the then Ministry of Transport; it is thousands of years old and central to all of the world's religious and ethical traditions. The Jewish scholar Hillel the Elder, a sage in the age of chariots, said the Old Testament could be boiled down to 'What is hateful to you, do not do to your fellow'. This cardinal rule is also in today's Highway Code: 'It is important that all road users are considerate towards each other.'

It could be argued that by dint of their greater horsepower and speed, those propelled by engines have more reason to show such consideration. And just as motorists have an abiding responsibility to look out for those not in motor vehicles, so cyclists, who can ride more quickly than walking pace, have a duty of care to look out for pedestrians. (By extension, faster pedestrians have to watch out for slower ones.)

I welcome the AA's *Cyclist's Highway Code*. It is practical, timely and useful – and it's also an indication that more and more people are taking up cycling, for transport, for leisure, and most definitely for pleasure.

Carlton Reid
Executive editor of *BikeBiz* magazine
Author of *Roads Were Not Built For Cars*

CYCLIST'S HIGHWAY CODE

Essential Rules of the Road

Published by AA Publishing (a trading name of AA Media Limited, whose registered office is Fanum House, Basing View, Basingstoke, Hampshire RG21 4EA; registered number 06112600).

© AA Media Limited 2016

Highway Code, National Standard for Cycle Training and road sign information licensed under the terms of the Open Government Licence v3.0, www.nationalarchives.gov.uk/doc/open-government-licence/version/3

Highway Code rules reproduced from *The Official Highway Code*, Department for Transport and the Driver and Vehicle Standards Agency, © Crown copyright 2015. The rules may be updated during the currency of this book – www.gov.uk/guidance/the-highway-code/updates

National Standard for Cycle Training levels 1–3 reproduced from Department of Transport documents at www.bikeability.org.uk/publications

Road signs, signals and markings reproduced from *Know Your Traffic Signs*, Department for Transport, © Crown copyright 2007.

The Bikeability logo (page 97) is a Crown copyright property.

Pages 8–25, 29, 31, 33–34, 36–37, 40–41 and 124–125 by Lara Dunn.

Design: Kat Mead
Verification: Carlton Reid
Proofreader: Kim Davies
Indexer: Marie Lorimer

ISBN 978-0-7495-7810-7

A05418

Printed in China by 1010 International

Visit AA Publishing at theAA.com/shop

Credits & acknowledgements

All images are sourced from The Automobile Association's Image Library except the following:

Cover composite: Route55/Alamy & YAY Media AS/Alamy

7 Blend Images/Alamy; 19 John Warburton-Lee Photography/Alamy; 20 Maskot/Alamy; 21 Arterra Picture Library/Alamy; 22 Birgitte Mejer/Alamy; 23 Brian Atkinson/Alamy; 27 MITO images/Alamy; 30 Tom King/Alamy; 35 Ian Shaw/Alamy; 36 incamerastock/Alamy; 41 format4/Alamy; 53 redsnapper/Alamy; 97 Mark Ferguson/Alamy

Every effort has been made to trace the copyright holders, and we apologise in advance for any unintentional omissions or errors. We would be pleased to apply any corrections in any following edition of this publication.

Introduction

The AA has been involved in cycling since our foundation in 1905. Our first patrols (or scouts) used cycles and in the First World War AA employees made up two companies of the 8th (Cyclist) Battalion of the Essex Regiment.

More recently our award-winning 'Think Bikes' side-mirror sticker campaign – inspired by AA patrol Tony Rich, and promoted by the AA Trust – to remind drivers to look out for cyclists, has gone global and is now running in 24 countries.

We work closely with former Olympic champion and British Cycling policy adviser Chris Boardman, and the AA was one of the first businesses to sign up to the #ChooseCycling network, which highlights the role cycling can play in helping businesses thrive by encouraging people to live healthier lives. As Chris Boardman says 'The bicycle is such a simple tool, but one which can improve your health, reduce congestion and make our towns and cities more liveable.'

This guide is intended for new cyclists and parents of children learning to ride. It includes sections on Your Bike (buying a bike, cycle care), Safe Cycling (all the essential Highway Code rules) and Learning to Ride (cycle training).

I am grateful to cycling expert Carlton Reid, executive editor of *BikeBiz* magazine, who has helped to check this publication in terms of good advice and accuracy.

Finally, as a keen cyclist and father of three cycling children, I would urge you to check out this book. Cyclists and drivers are often the same people. Today more than one fifth of AA members regularly cycle and this guide will encourage a new generation to join them.

Edmund King OBE
AA President

Your Bike

Whether you and your family are new to cycling or you're getting back on a bike after several years, it's always good to refresh your knowledge. This section looks at the essentials you need to get started.

A family pursuit

Cycling is a fun activity that children love, and teaching your child to ride a bike and going on family cycling trips are rewarding experiences. Not only is cycling a great way to travel, but as a regular form of exercise it can make an invaluable contribution to a child's health and fitness, and increase their sense of independence. See pages 8–9 for advice on choosing a child's bike and pages 16–17 for ways of transporting very young children on two wheels. Once children are at school, they may have the opportunity to do cycle training – see pages 96–121 for a guide to the National Standard for Cycling Training.

Preparing your bicycle

Like any machine, a bike will work better and last longer if you care for it properly. Get in the habit of checking your bike regularly – simple checks and maintenance can help you enjoy hassle-free riding and avoid repairs. See pages 20–25 for a list of common problems you might encounter.

A basic routine includes checking the wheels for broken spokes or excess play in the bearings, and checking the tyres for punctures, undue wear and the correct tyre pressures. Ensure that the brake blocks are firmly in place and not worn, and that cables are not frayed or too slack. Lubricate hubs, pedals, gear mechanisms and cables. Make sure you have a pump, a bell, a rear rack to carry panniers and, if cycling at night, a set of working lights.

Look after your bike and your bike will look after you – regular care will keep your machine in top condition for hassle-free riding

Buying a Bike

Choosing Bikes for Children

Getting the right bike for a junior rider is a crucial step in helping to create an enjoyable lifelong relationship with cycling. While a child may be taken in by a bike's colour or by character-marketing ploys, the parent is left with the trickier job of working out the correct size and the right bike for the type of riding that the child will be doing.

First decide if the bike is going to be mainly used on-road or whether it needs to be suitable for all-terrain. Most bikes designed for riders aged four to ten years old will either be all-terrain mountain-bike-style bikes, or BMX bikes, with the specialisation increasing with age. A child may well have a strong preference for one or the other. From about nine years old upwards, junior road bikes also become an option. With 24" wheels, these can be a good first step for future road enthusiasts.

Flashing LEDs
Great for adding safety for the young rider, these are inexpensive and available in a huge variety of fun options, allowing for customisation of the bike. The same is true of reflective stickers and spoke lights.

Brakes
Making sure a child's bike has good-quality and effective brakes that can be safely and easily operated by smaller hands can make a big difference to a child's confidence.

Accessories
As with adult bikes, children's bicycles are legally required to be fitted with a bell and front and rear reflectors, but only if the bike is purchased as new. Most junior riders would probably much prefer to choose from the wealth of cool aftermarket bell designs available! Mudguards are a sensible addition to any child's bike where they are not fitted as standard.

Sizing

Choosing the correct size for a child can be tricky, but most manufacturers base advice on wheel size as a rough guide.

2 – 5 years	4 – 8 years	7 – 10 years	10 upwards
Wheel size: 12"	Wheel size: 16"	Wheel size: 20"	Either a 24" wheel or even a small adult bike 20" – depends on confidence
Balance bikes	Pedal bikes	Pedal bikes	

It's not an exact science as children often don't fall within the required size parameters, but if they're comfortable and can control the bike, chances are it's the right size.

Seat height

Many better-quality junior bikes come with longer than average seatposts to allow for rapid growth and constant adjustment. Adjusting the height of the saddle is a quick and easy job, particularly if it's fastened with a 'quick-release' skewer. The child should feel comfortable and safe, but in an ideal world, knees should be almost straight at full extension on the pedals.

Gears

Can complicate cycling for early riders so a single speed should be enough. For older children, three gears should be sufficient until they become more confident in their riding.

Stabilisers

Current practice favours balance bikes in preference to more traditional stabilisers for early riders; they encourage better balance and confidence in a child, which can be carried through to proper cycling without the extra psychological hurdle of removing the stabilisers.

Choosing a Bike for Adults

Buying the right adult bike is probably significantly harder than choosing one for a child. The choice is near endless and the price range staggering, so it's really important to have a good long think about requirements before even setting foot in a shop. At that point, a test ride of a few contenders is a good idea.

First decide if the bike is going to be mainly for on road, off-road or all-terrain, or for something specific. Also, decide the type of riding that's going to be most applicable, such as fitness, racing, long distances, transport, commuting or recreation. A hybrid, suited to most terrains and most types of riding, can be an easy option for those wanting a do-everything bike. Hybrid bikes usually have straight handlebars, wider tyres and often disc brakes. They also usually feature mudguards and sometimes even a rear rack.

TOP TIP

Think carefully about the main purpose of your cycling. This will help you buy the most appropriate style for your needs.

Saddle

An incredibly personal part of the bike, you may want to change this after purchase for one of the correct width and firmness for comfort. A professional 'saddle fit' is a good idea. Saddle height is easily adjusted, particularly if a quick-release skewer is used on the seat tube.

Gears

Either lever shift or twist shift, these vary in number between one (single speed) and currently around 27, although this number will doubtless go up soon. The important thing is not so much the number of gears as the usefulness of the set-up, how smooth the gear transition is and the suitability to the type of terrain that will be tackled.

Sizing

There's no hard and fast rule for sizing of adult bikes as each manufacturer can take a different approach. Take advice from a bike shop, go for a few test rides on different models and brands and build up an idea of what suits you best. Unisex, mens' bikes and womens' bikes vary enormously in sizing too. Tall- or medium-height women may find either type suits, while shorter women may be better off looking at female-specific models.

Style

Adult bikes come in as many different styles as sizes and colours, from laid-back cruiser types, to folding bikes, and sporty road machines, shopping bikes or upright models. Mens' bikes mostly have straight top tubes and womens' bikes have a dropped top tube. However, a woman rider can ride a so-called man's bike or vice versa, if it's comfortable and the correct size.

Brakes

Mountain bikes usually come with hydraulic disc brakes, which are easy to pull on and very effective. Hybrids can be equipped with rim brakes or mechanical disc brakes, with the latter being more effective but requiring more maintenance. Road bikes are most frequently equipped with rim brakes, although disc brakes are starting to become more common on high-end models.

Accessories

New adult bikes are legally required to be fitted with a bell and front and rear reflectors at the point of sale. Mudguards are a sensible addition to hybrid, touring or recreational bikes where they are not fitted as standard, and detachable ones for mountain or road bikes are handy. A rear rack can be useful if you need to carry luggage.

Key Accessories

The Essentials

There's a bewildering, and seemingly ever-expanding, selection of gadgets and gizmos available on the market for kitting out both bike and rider, ranging in price from pennies to hundreds of pounds. All the essentials are easily available, however, and don't have to cost the earth to increase safety on the road and enhance ride enjoyment.

Bell

All bikes purchased as new in the UK will come with a bell as a legal requirement. There is a world of difference between the basic sort of bell that comes free with a new bike and some of the gloriously sonorous bicycle jewellery available. Prices vary hugely, but so does build quality, attractiveness and even volume of ding. When many pedestrians are wearing headphones, it's good to know a bell is loud.

Lights

A decent set of front and back lights is one of the most important investments that can be made for cycling safety. A good set of LED lights costs around £20, although more expensive lights are brighter and more robust. Less expensive lights won't be as bright, will have shorter lifespans and may be prone to technical or environmental faults, making them a false economy.

Flashing LED light

Although the flashing element is usually a setting of continuous LED lights, a flashing light can be a cheap way to add extra visibility, beyond the bright headlights, or on their own for added daytime safety. They are usually inexpensive, and frequently clip on either to bike or rider in a variety of ingenious ways. They are available in novelty options and different shapes and can be a fun way for children to jazz up their bikes too.

TOP TIP »»»»»» Lights are a common target for thieves – take them with you after securing your bike. The same goes for all other detachable accessories.

Reflectors

These also come fitted, front and back, as a legal requirement on new bikes in the UK, but a variety of more attractive ones are available such as snowflake shapes. Enhancing after-dark visibility is vital for safety, and wheel-mounted reflectors are cheap and effective, if only from the sides. Reflectors are red at the back, white at the front.

Pump

Modern lightweight pumps are not only compact, light and easy to carry on the bike, but are often maximised to make the act of pumping up a tyre less hard work. A CO2 cannister style pump, originating in the mountain biking world, can make the job even easier, with a simple cartridge doing the worst of the work.

Lock

These can be bike mounted, rider worn or just thrown into a bag or pannier. The key is to allocate as much budget as possible, with the Sold Secure approval label being a good thing to look for as an indicator of build quality and security. Sold Secure Silver and Gold are very reliable locks and are available in a range of weights and lengths.

Other Key Accessories

Repair kit
A spare inner tube is by far the easiest option, but taking along some self-adhesive tyre patches is also a good idea, just in case the puncture strikes both front and back. Tyre levers will be needed too.

Tool kit/multi-tool
Small and preferably light-weight, a cycling-specific multi-tool will usually feature the more frequently required tools, such as popular sized Allen keys, screwdrivers, chain-breaking tool and a spoke wrench.

Reflectives
These are a great way to add visibility after dark or in low light. They range from tabards and vests to chest and ankle straps. Also available, however, are more quirky and fun options such as badges, scarves, hats, shoes and stickers for both bike and rider, all of which have a reflective element to them. It's even possible to buy a fully reflective waterproof jacket. Never assume that because you have enough light to see, you can be seen by other road users.

TOP TIP
Always carry a mobile phone with you. It could be invaluable if you are stuck without a repair kit and need help.

Water bottle and holder

Mounting a bottle cage on the frame of the bike is the most straightforward and easy way of carrying a sports water bottle to avoid dehydration when riding. Some retro and vintage bikes have handlebar-mounted water-bottle carriers and it's possible to get them for behind the saddle too.

Seat pouch

A small pouch that straps behind the saddle is an excellent place to keep a toolkit and spare inner tube and, depending on its size, even house keys and perhaps a snack. Designs, sizes and prices are incredibly varied, with a choice to suit every style and budget. These are often also a perfect place to mount an extra rear LED light.

Computer

Not strictly required, but these vary in price from a few pounds at a supermarket for something that just calculates speed, distance and time, to hundreds of pounds for a GPS-enabled device that does everything. The main difference between simple cycle computers and GPS-enabled devices is that a GPS can not only deliver ride statistics, but also has mapping and navigation capability and can assist with training plans. These require no setting up, unlike cycle computers, and can be switched between bikes. It's worth noting that smartphones can also be attached to bikes and there are apps that will do all of the above jobs.

TOP TIP Do your homework before buying expensive equipment – online consumer reviews and blogs are a good source of information.

Riding with Young Children

Travelling with Kids

Riding safely with children is easier than ever before. This is primarily thanks to the constant innovation that has come about as a result of the growth in popularity of cycling. Parents and guardians can now choose how to carry their child based on age and size, as well as the parents' individual requirements.

Front- and rear-mounted child seats

Traditional rear bike-mounted child seats are very popular, and are the cheapest option and most suitable for very small children, from about six months to five years old. Front-mounted seats that perch between the rider and the handlebars are also available, giving the child a better view and allowing the parent to keep a watchful eye on their little passenger. These are suitable for children from one year. Both styles of child seat vary hugely in both cost and quality, but well-made models are a definite cut above the plain hard plastic bucket seats of the past, with a substantial increase in safety and ease of use. Some designs even offer a reclining option to make the most of the fact that small children often fall asleep on bikes.

Cargo bikes

Cargo bikes are becoming increasingly popular among urban-based cycling families. Popular in Denmark and the Netherlands, these bicycles feature an integrated cargo area for load carrying. In their simplest form they can carry groceries and the like, but some are designed with child transport in mind, making it easy for a parent to see the child at all times, since they sit at the front rather than being towed behind. Sturdy and heavy to ride, even when empty, these are best suited to flat, urban environments. They are suitable from birth to adulthood.

A rear-mounted child seat

A front-mounted child seat

Trailer bikes

For those with children old enough to want to ride their own bike, from about four years old to nine, a tag-a-long, also known as a 'trailer bike' fastens onto an adult bike. They are effectively half a bike, with pedals, a chain and sometimes even gears. Fortunately, for the rider at the front, they do not feature brakes or steering. A tag-a-long can be a good way of including a child in longer family rides, while increasing their fitness endurance and road sense without overtiring them.

Trailers

Trailers are a significantly higher investment than a child seat. They can, however, be a good option for those wanting to transport multiple children, and they allow for a wide variety of ages, from six months to six years or so. Attaching at the back, they can require practice to be able to manoeuvre with confidence, but many of the higher-spec models include safety features such as brakes and even roll cages, and all give good protection from the elements.

TOP TIP
Before buying a trailer, think ahead. How much use will you and your child get out of it? Are they old enough for their own bike?

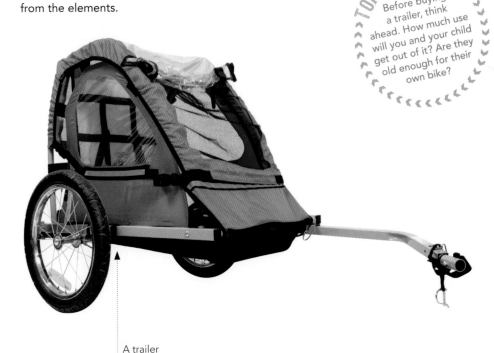

A trailer

Family cycling

Beyond the practicalities of actually how to take a child out cycling, it's worth considering how to make a family ride as enjoyable an experience as possible.

Be prepared

- **Plan your trip** around interesting stops and sights along the way. Don't make journey times any longer than children are happy to sit and play at home. An off-road route such as one at a family cycling centre keeps thing relaxed and safe.
- **Take extra clothes and waterproofs** – just in case. Children are less weather aware and less able to control their own temperature, so parents will want to pack some extra clothing layers. Check that trousers and laces can't get caught in the chain when pedalling along. Wrap up toddlers. When a young child is on the back of a bike, they won't be generating heat like the person doing all the pedalling!
- **Take along snacks, water and treats** to keep their energy and spirit levels up.
- **Carry some sticking plasters and antiseptic wipes** – kids are far more likely to fall off and graze arms, hands or knees.
- **Don't be too ambitious.** It's much better that everyone wants to go out again, than all coming home exhausted, tearful and permanently put off cycling.

Be safe

- **Checking a child's bike over** before any ride is a good idea, but if a trailer, tag-a-long or bike seat are involved, it's crucial to check the adult's bike too.
- **Check your bike over** for any damage or mechanical faults. Do the brakes and gears work? Is the saddle the right height? Are the tyres pumped up?
- **Adopt good helmet practice.** In adulthood wearing a helmet is a personal choice, but for a child a helmet should be a way of life. A helmet should fit snugly and properly and be worn just above the eyebrows, not on the back of the head. Be careful not to pinch their skin when buckling the helment strap. It's easily done and often ends in tears. Just place your forefinger between the strap and the chin.

On the ride

- **Maintain chat with young riders** to check how they are feeling and to keep them from straying into overtiredness.
- **Ride in a line with the children in the middle** of the adults. If there's only one of you, the adult should be at the rear, keeping an eye on all the children in front.
- **Treats can be an incentive** if there's only a short distance left to the end, and the child is flagging.

Enjoy your riding

- **At the end of a ride,** enjoying a hot chocolate or cake can reinforce the positive experience of being out as a family.
- **Take photos,** while stationary, to record the trip.

Cycle Care

10 Common Problems (and How to Avoid Them)

1 Punctures

An annoying thing to happen mid-ride is to get a puncture. There are a few common causes for punctured tyres that are easy to avoid. Keep them pumped up to the pressure stated by the manufacturer on the side of the tyre. Insufficiently inflated tyres are more prone to punctures and 'pinch flats' where the inner tube gets compressed against the wheel wall. Repeat punctures can be avoided by checking the inside of the tyre for the original cause. Some thorns embed themselves so firmly that they keep on deflating tyres.

Taking along a puncture repair kit on any ride is a good idea. A small hand pump, a spare inner tube and tyre levers are all that's required really, but for additional roadside repairs, stick-on patches are a bonus.

TOP TIP If in doubt, leave it to the professionals. Some will even collect the bike from your home or office and return it when done.

It used to be that regular punctures were an inevitability of riding a bike. Now, thanks to special toughened tyres and self-sealing products that can be put inside inner tubes to help seal a puncture, they can be a lot easier to avoid, provided that basic maintenance checks are regularly performed. See pages 24–25 for a step-by-step guide to mending a puncture.

Regular checks

Carry out the following checks to keep your bike well maintained and in good working order.
Every week:
- Check tyres, brakes, lights, handlebars and seat are in good order and tightly secured.
- Wipe clean and lubricate chain.
- Wipe the dirt from wheels.
- Check tread on tyres.
- Check brake pads.
- Check gear and brake cables and make sure that gears are changing smoothly.

Every year:
- Take your bike to an cycle mechanic for a thorough service.

2 Gear shift issues

This is usually down to over-stretched, slackened gear cables. These can be adjusted on a day-to-day basis, if required by use of the barrel adjuster at the gear shifter on the bars, or the one at the cable itself. However, gear cables need to be changed every now and again to keep everything running smoothly and efficiently. It's an inexpensive and fairly straightforward job. Another reason for occasional cable changes is that over time, the cables can draw moisture and muck inside, resulting in stiff gear changes, and bad shifts.

3 Bottom soreness

Some new cyclists complain of sore or chafed backsides, but it is avoidable. The most important thing is a correctly proportioned saddle that suits both the width of the rider's sitbones, where most of the weight sits, and his or her riding style. Getting the saddle in the right place will help you get the most from your pedal power without strain. Many bike shops can assist with a saddle-fitting service. It is also crucial to have the saddle at the correct height and angle for prolonged comfort (although this will depend on the type of bike and the type of riding). A well-fitting pair of good-quality padded cycling shorts are a worthy investment and should always be worn with no underwear. For long rides, or in hot conditions, it's a good idea to consider an anti-chafing chamois cream.

4 Numb or uncomfortable hands

Aside from replacing handlebar grips or tape with a more cushioned variety, padded cycling gloves can help prevent soreness on the palms and also help alleviate the pressure on the ulnar nerve of the hand, which can cause numbness and tingling. If the problem persists, it's worth getting a proper bike fit done with a specialist. Failing that, see a doctor.

TOP TIP Don't ignore any pain you feel when riding – if it's not a problem with your bike then you should seek medical attention.

10 Common Problems (and How to Avoid Them)

5 Sore knees

This is usually down to a seat being positioned too low (or less often, too high). The centre of the pedal spindle should sit directly under the knee cap when the pedals are in a horizontal position, and the leg should be almost straight, but never hyper-extended, at the bottom-most part of the pedal rotation. It's also important to check that both feet are roughly straight on the pedals, not turned in or out.

6 Noisy or ineffective brakes

Poor adjustment or wearing of the brake pads can cause both squealing and inefficiency of braking power. Check cable rim brakes regularly and adjust so that they are correctly centred for maximum contact when needed. The barrel adjuster for finer tuning may be mounted on the handlebars, at the brake lever, or may be on the frame or the brake itself. Cable disc brakes are complex so seek the help of a bike shop.

7 Rusty chain

By cleaning the chain regularly (every week or so) and lubricating afterwards, it's possible to avoid rust. Chain cleaning devices make this an easy job – with small brushes and a reservoir for a cleaning product, they keep the worst of the mess contained and are very effective. Rinse the chain after cleaning, then run it through a cloth or piece of sturdy kitchen towel to dry, before applying a specialist bike lubricant every couple of links, while constantly rotating pedals to help distribute it properly. Modern bike lubricants are a much more effective option than light oils such as 3-in-1 oil. If there is insufficient time to clean a chain fully before a ride, running it through a cloth soaked in a little lubricant does a good temporary job. A desperately rusty chain may need to be removed from the bike and soaked in an oil bath to help loosen up the links.

8 Chain marks on leg

These usually come about as a result of tilting the bike at junctions and stops. Making sure the chain is not overlubricated by wiping off excess after application can help, but it often happens anyway. The only fool-proof way to avoid the 'cyclist's tattoo' is to use a chain guard. These don't fit or suit all bikes, but for many town bikes and touring bikes they are a godsend. They can be fitted after market to some bike styles. The best way to remove the oil mark is with something like Vaseline, a make-up cleansing wipe or even sugar.

9 Worn chain rings

This can result in bad gear changes, or even the chain getting stuck or jammed when changing gear. As the chain wears over time, it stretches, wearing the teeth of the chain rings more on one side than the other. This slowly causes the teeth to get hooked and can catch on the chain, which can then stick. Worst-case scenario, the chain can come off and get caught between the chain rings and the bike, causing an almost immediate stop. It is worth visually inspecting the chain rings for wear every now and then, and replacing them, along with the chain.

10 Chain keeps coming off

This can be caused by worn chain rings or a rusty chain (see points 7 and 9 above), but it can also be the result of a poorly adjusted end stop on the gearing, meaning that the chain can simply 'hop off' at the end points. Having a chain that constantly comes off can also be an indicator that it has stretched and slackened somewhat, showing age and wear. At this point it is worth checking the chain rings for wear as well and considering a replacement. Your local bike shop can assist with fitting one.

Repairing a Puncture

Out on a ride, it's often easier to replace a damaged inner tube with a fresh spare than attempt roadside puncture repairs with a repair kit and patches. Repairing inner tubes is a job best done in a comfortable chair with a cup of tea. Nonetheless, the process of taking the wheel off, replacing the damaged tube, reseating it and pumping it up again are all the same whichever course of action is chosen.

1 Remove the wheel, tyre and tube

Start by removing the wheel. Let any remaining air out of the inner tube using the valve. Insert the blunt end of one of the tyre levers between the tyre and the wheel rim. Lever the edge of the tyre over the rim and hook the lever's other end around a spoke. Insert a second tyre lever under the tyre rim and push around the rim to lift it off, then remove the inner tube. If the tyre is tight on the rim, you might need to use a third tyre lever.

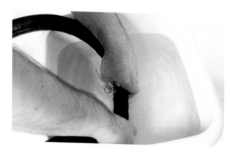

2 Check the tyre

Lift the tyre completely off the wheel and inspect the inside surface for any cuts or foreign objects that might have caused the puncture. Carefully running fingers round is a one way to find anything, but be careful. A deeply cut tyre will need replacing. Any thorns, tacks or foreign objects found lodged in the tyre can be pulled out from the outside. Use needle-nose pliers.

3 Locate the hole

Inflate the damaged tube and locate the puncture by rotating it, listening closely for the hiss of escaping air (or put the tube in water and watch for bubbles). Mark the location with the repair kit's wax stick (note, there may be more than one hole). Deflate the tube fully and apply a self-adhesive patch carefully.

Equipment

1. Pump
2. Tyre levers (2 or 3)
3. Patches
4. Tweezers/needle-nose pliers

TOP TIP »»»»»

To ensure a patch fully adheres, make sure all wrinkles are smoothed out.

4 Apply a patch

If using a traditional repair kit with non-adhesive patches, roughen the tube-surface with sandpaper, select a patch and spread a thin layer of glue slightly larger than the patch over the roughened area. Allow the glue to go tacky, then firmly press the patch onto the glue, ensuring that the edges are flat. Apply pressure for about a minute, then use the abrasive to grind chalk onto the repair to stop excess glue issues.

5 Replace the tube and tyre

Put one side of the tyre on the rim. Inflate the tube slightly to give some shape, and push the valve down through the hole in the wheel rim. Work the tube around, onto the rim under the tyre. Push the valve upwards slightly and lift the other side of the tyre over the rim. Work the rest of the tyre back onto the rim. Using tyre levers is a last resort.

6 Pump up and replace wheel

Massage the tyre around gently to ensure nothing is pinching the tube and it is positioned evenly, then pump up to the pressure quoted on the tyre wall. Refit the wheel onto the bike, making sure any quick-release skewers are well secured, and brakes are returned to operational position.

Repairing a Puncture   25

Safe Cycling

This section features the cycling-related rules of *The Highway Code* for England, Scotland and Wales. *The Highway Code* is essential reading and provides key information for all road users and applies to pedestrians and cyclists as much as to car drivers and motorcycle riders.

Rules for cyclists

The main rules for cyclists are covered by Rules 59 to 82 and Annexe 1 of *The Highway Code*. In this section they sit alongside other related parts of the Code, which also apply to all vehicles. The Code's rules have been reordered, but the original rule numbers are clearly marked and the rules sit between dotted red lines. Many include an abbreviated reference to the relevant legislation (page 126). Rules that use 'MUST/MUST NOT' are legal requirements. Some rules have been summarised and extra, non-Highway Code, text has been provided for advice only.

Knowing the rules

Knowing and applying the rules in *The Highway Code* could significantly reduce road casualties. The rules do not give cyclists and motorists the right of way in any circumstance, but they do advise when road users should give way to others. Always give way if it can help to avoid an incident.

Read the road and be prepared

Adapt your riding to the appropriate type and condition of road you are on. In particular, take the road and traffic conditions into account. Be prepared for unexpected or difficult situations, for example, the road being blocked beyond a blind bend. Be prepared to adjust your speed as a precaution and try to anticipate what other people and vehicles on the road might do. If pedestrians, particularly children, are looking the other way, they may step out into the road without seeing you. Be considerate towards all road users, especially those requiring extra care

The Highway Code is essential reading for all road users. Here, we present all the main rules relevant to cyclists.

(see pages 54–59). Above all, you must not ride dangerously, ride without due care and attention or ride without reasonable consideration for other road users.

ANNEXE

1 **You and your bicycle.** Make sure that you feel confident of your ability to ride safely on the road. Be sure that

- you choose the right size and type of cycle for comfort and safety
- lights and reflectors are kept clean and in good working order
- tyres are in good condition and inflated to the pressure shown on the tyre
- gears are working correctly
- the chain is properly adjusted and oiled
- the saddle and handlebars are adjusted to the correct height.

It is recommended that you fit a bell to your cycle.

You **MUST**

- ensure your brakes are efficient
- at night, use lit front and rear lights and have a red rear reflector.
  Laws PCUR regs 6 & 10 & RVLR reg 18

Clothing

059 **Clothing.** You should wear
- a cycle helmet which conforms to current regulations, is the correct size and securely fastened
- appropriate clothes for cycling. Avoid clothes that may get tangled in the chain, or in a wheel or may obscure your lights
- light-coloured or fluorescent clothing which helps other road users to see you in daylight and poor light
- reflective clothing and/or accessories (belt, arm or ankle bands) in the dark.

Rule 59: Help yourself to be seen

Be safe and be seen

Any clothing can be used for cycling, but it's best to avoid loose garments that can flap about or get caught in the bike and to take care that dresses or coats don't cover and obscure rear lights or reflectors. Items in bright or lighter colours can be more visible to other road users, and high-visibility super-bright colours, frequently used for cycling jackets and clothing, are better still for drawing attention.

Helmets

Safety standards for cycling helmets are fairly stringently enforced since the UK adopted the European General Safety Product Regulations, which forbid the marketing of unsafe products. The vast majority of helmets on sale should therefore conform to a reputable standard like EN1078 and be marked as such. A cycling helmet should fit well and be comfortable. One indication of a good fit is if the wearer can tip the head right forwards and the helmet stays put even with the chin strap unfastened. Position is important, with the optimal distance being about a finger's width between the helmet and the eyebrows, not tilted backwards or forwards. Size adjustments should be made where possible, according to the helmet design, to ensure a secure fit. Straps should be adjusted to sit snug against the head and chin, but not be too tight.

Reflective accessories

Reflective accents on clothing and gloves are extremely beneficial for low light conditions, and can be augmented by the addition of reflective accessories such as chest straps, ankle bands, stickers, badges, scarves and the like. There are even a few fully reflective jackets available, which are super-visible in car headlights, but quite a dull silver grey in natural light.

Some cycle-specific jackets come with a stick-on flashing LED light strip or possibly a loop on the back to hang any clip-on lightweight LED light from. These are a useful way to further boost low light visibility.

At Night

The *Highway Code* defines night, or the hours of darkness, as 'the period between half an hour after sunset and half an hour before sunrise'.

RULE
060 **At night** your cycle MUST have white front and red rear lights lit. It MUST also be fitted with a red rear reflector (and amber pedal reflectors, if manufactured after 1/10/85). White front reflectors and spoke reflectors will also help you to be seen. Flashing lights are permitted but it is recommended that cyclists who are riding in areas without street lighting use a steady front lamp.
Law RVLR regs 13, 18 & 24

Cycling after dark

Reflectors and reflectives are an important part of a cyclist's after-dark toolkit. It's worth bearing in mind that although new bikes are legally required to come with reflectors fitted as standard, this is not the case with secondhand bikes so you should ensure that you fit them.

After dark, or in low or fading light, front and rear lights are crucial. Although there may be enough light to see by, there may not be enough to BE SEEN. Flashing LEDs are useful and visible but preferably as an addition to a steady beam light. Lights should be bright, clean and well maintained and the rider should be confident that there is sufficient battery life for the whole journey.

LED lights use significantly less power than standard bulbs for their brightness, meaning increased battery life, but they vary hugely in terms of brightness, power consumption and cost. Given that a front and rear light are absolutely pivotal in making a rider visible after dark, it makes sense to spend as much as budget allows to purchase lights that are absolutely as bright as possible, yet have a good battery life and build quality. Some lights even come with additional battery packs that can be taken along on long rides just in case and many feature a battery warning indicator. A useful feature to look for in a front light is illuminated sections on the side wall of the light body. This makes the light visible from the sides as well, making it safer at junctions.

Riding at night requires good awareness of other road users and pedestrians, who may not be visible. In turn, it is further hampered by reduced vision and depth perception. Extra care should be taken at junctions, particularly when turning right. Reflective straps or LEDs on gloves or forearm can help make signalling more obvious.

Small LED flashers are an excellent way to enhance low light and after dark visibility. These can be attached to clothing, a bag or pack or to the bike itself. Red should be used for rear-facing surfaces and white for front-facing.

Cycle Routes, Tracks & Lanes

Cycle routes

See also page 35 for rules associated with these facilities.

See also page 35 for rules associated with these facilities.

RULE
061 Cycle routes and other facilities. Use cycle routes, advanced stop lines, cycle boxes and toucan crossings unless at the time it is unsafe to do so. Use of these facilities is not compulsory and will depend on your experience and skills, but they can make your journey safer.

Cycle tracks

See page 35 for rules about cycle lanes.

RULE
062 Cycle tracks. These are normally located away from the road, but may occasionally be found alongside footpaths or pavements. Cyclists and pedestrians may be segregated or they may share the same space (unsegregated). When using segregated tracks you MUST keep to the side intended for cyclists as the pedestrian side remains a pavement or footpath. Take care when passing pedestrians, especially children, older or disabled people, and allow them plenty of room. Always be prepared to slow down and stop if necessary. Take care near road junctions as you may have difficulty seeing other road users, who might not notice you.
Law HA 1835 sect 72

Cycle tracks: a pedestrian's point of view

The 'Rules for Pedestrians' section of *The Highway Code* advises:

RULE
013 Routes shared with cyclists. Some cycle tracks run alongside footpaths or pavements, using a segregating feature to separate cyclists from people on foot. Segregated routes may also incorporate short lengths of tactile paving to help visually impaired people stay on the correct side. On the pedestrian side this will comprise a series of flat-topped bars running across the direction of travel (ladder pattern). On the cyclist side the same bars are orientated in the direction of travel (tramline pattern). Not all routes which are shared with cyclists are segregated. Take extra care where this is so (see Rule 62 above).

 Reminder to pedestrians to look out for pedal cycles approaching from the right

 Shared route for pedal cycles and pedestrians only

 Separated track and path for pedal cycles and pedestrians

Using cycle ways

There are a variety of types of cycle path and track. These can each require a different approach from the cyclist using them. For convenience, they can be split into two groups – designated cycle ways and non-designated cycle ways.

Direction signs specifically for cyclists have a blue background and include a white pedal-cycle symbol. Most are free-standing signs, but some primary and non-primary route-direction signs may incorporate a blue panel indicating a route for cyclists that is different from that for other traffic. The cycle symbol may also be used on pedestrian signs where cyclists and pedestrians share the route.

| Route for pedal cycles only | Riding of pedal cycles prohibited | Road marking separating cyclists and pedestrians on a shared route (may be a raised line up to 20mm high) |

Designated cycle ways are usually part of an established road or footpath network and either run as a section of the pavement or as a section of the road (see pages 36–37). These are usually clearly signposted, either painted on the road or pavement surface itself or at intervals alongside on marker posts. Pedestrians and cyclists may be segregated on pavement cycle ways or they may share the same space.

Non-designated cycle ways are made up principally of bridleways and unsurfaced tracks defined as 'byways'. Bridleways are usually marked with a signpost while byways may be unmarked. These are usually best researched first using an Ordnance Survey map or guidebook.

- **Only ride where it is legal to do so.** It is forbidden to cycle on public footpaths unless they are clearly marked as shared-use paths, usually with a blue sign. The only non-designated 'rights of way' open to cyclists are bridleways and unsurfaced tracks, known as byways, which are open to all traffic.

Pedal cyclists to dismount at end of, or break in, a cycle lane, track or route

End of cycle lane, track or route

Road marking indicating the end of a cycle lane, track or route

- **On cycle ways shared with pedestrians**, always keep to the side intended for cyclists. The other side remains a footpath and therefore out of bounds. Care should be taken when passing pedestrians, particularly children, the elderly or disabled, or those with dogs. Allow them plenty of space. Take care at road junctions and crossing points and always be aware of other road and cycle way users. Be aware that cycle lanes on roads may require interaction with vehicular traffic and navigation of complex road systems. Marked cycle lanes may also finish unexpectedly, requiring a return to normal road use.
- **Canal towpaths:** these are not rights of way, rather permissive paths where cycling is allowed by the Canal & River Trust (www.canalrivertrust.org.uk), but only within their guidelines. Remember that towpaths can sometimes be closed for maintenance and access paths can be steep and slippery. Bikes are best pushed by hand rather than ridden under low bridges and by locks.
- **Always yield to walkers and horses**, giving adequate warning of approach.
- **Keep to the main trail** to avoid any unnecessary erosion to surrounding areas and to prevent skidding, especially if it is wet.
- **Remember the Countryside Code** (www.gov.uk/government/publications/the-countryside-code).
- **Do not expect to cycle at high speed** on any cycle path or cycle way.

Cycle lanes

RULE
063 **Cycle lanes.** These are marked by a white line (which may be broken) along the carriageway. Keep within the lane when practicable. When leaving a cycle lane check before pulling out that it is safe to do so and signal your intention clearly to other road users. Use of cycle lanes is not compulsory and will depend on your experience and skills, but they can make your journey safer.

In the general rules section of *The Highway Code*, all road users are given very clear guidance on how to treat cycle lanes in rule 140.

RULE
140 **Cycle lanes** are shown by road markings and signs. You MUST NOT drive or park in a cycle lane marked by a solid white line during its times of operation. Do not drive or park in a cycle lane marked by a broken white line unless it is unavoidable. You MUST NOT park in any cycle lane whilst waiting restrictions apply.
Law RTRA sects 5 & 8

Pages 33–34 and 36–37 provide a selection of signs and road markings relating to cycle lanes.

Pages 82–89 provide advice on the use of crossings you might encounter on a cycle route (see Rule 81, page 83).

Cycle lanes are usually marked very clearly

Cycle Routes, Tracks & Lanes

Types of cycle lane

Mandatory cycle lanes – these are marked with a continuous white line. Due to the fact that cars should not drive, wait or park in these lanes during their hours of operation they are usually used only by cyclists. As these lanes attract larger numbers of cyclists, care should be taken when moving in a group with riders travelling at different speeds. Remain vigilant in case emergency braking is required.

Try to ride steadily and confidently and be aware that the lane may run out or divert from the desired direction. Stay aware of peripheral activity both within and outside of the cycle lane. When ready to leave the lane, check surrounding traffic, then indicate and move confidently.

Mandatory with-flow pedal cycle lane. Other vehicles must not use this part of the carriageway except to pick up or set down passengers. Hours of operation may be shown

Road markings for a mandatory pedal cycle lane

Mandatory with-flow pedal cycle lane ahead. Hours of operation may be shown

Research the cycle lanes in your area – you may be surprised how many you find

Advisory cycle lanes – these are marked by a broken white line. Care should be taken using these as the advice to cars only recommends that they should not enter the lane 'unless unavoidable'. Be aware of other riders and also of nearby motor traffic and always err on the side of caution in a situation requiring a split-second decision. Make sure indication of direction is clear and visible and move quickly and assertively to change position on the road as required. Be visible to all road users at all times.

Route recommended for pedal cycles on the main carriageway of a road. This may be marked as an advisory pedal cycle lane

Road markings for an advisory pedal cycle lane. Other vehicles should not use this part of the carriageway unless it is unavoidable

Contraflow cycle lanes – these allow cyclists to ride in the opposite direction to the main flow of traffic on a one-way street. They are party to the same rules for cars as mandatory cycle lanes. Where the cycle lane is a two-way lane, keep to the left. Be aware that the cycle lane may terminate at a point that requires rejoining a two-way road.

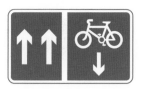

Mandatory contraflow pedal cycle lane (the upward arrows indicate the number of traffic lanes available)

Contraflow pedal cycles in a one-way street (other than a mandatory contraflow cycle lane). This may be marked by a broken line on the carriageway or there may be no line at all

Bus Lanes

RULE
065 Most bus lanes may be used by cyclists as indicated on signs. Watch out for people getting on or off a bus. Be very careful when overtaking a bus or leaving a bus lane as you will be entering a busier traffic flow. Do not pass between the kerb and a bus when it is at a stop.

RULE
141 **Bus lanes.** These are shown by road markings and signs that indicate which (if any) other vehicles are permitted to use the bus lane. Unless otherwise indicated, you should not drive in a bus lane during its period of operation. You may enter a bus lane to stop, to load or unload where this is not prohibited.

Shared bus and cycle lanes – these allow cyclists to use the same lane as buses. Cars should not enter these lanes during their hours of operation. Take extra care passing stationary buses and NEVER squeeze past a bus, either stationary or moving slowly, on the left. The blind spot for a bus's mirrors is large enough to lose several cyclists in. Buses stop frequently and there's an added hazard of them driving at slow speeds, so extreme caution is required when cycling in a bus lane. Be clearly visible out in the carriageway and move with the bus traffic rather than trying to overtake.

With-flow bus lane ahead that can also be used by pedal cycles and taxis. Hours of operation may be shown

With-flow bus and pedal cycle lane sign showing hours of operation

Route for buses and pedal cycles only (cycles not admitted when cycle symbol not shown; taxis admitted when 'taxi' shown in upper sign)

Road marking indicating the start of a route for buses only. TAXI and/ or the cycle symbol may be included

Bus-lane road marking

Traffic may use both lanes at the end of a bus lane

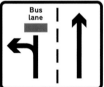

Where there is a break in a bus lane at a junction, other traffic may use the left-hand lane for turning left only

 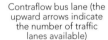

Contraflow bus lane (the upward arrows indicate the number of traffic lanes available)	Contraflow bus and pedal cycle lane on road at junction ahead	Road marking for a contraflow bus lane that is also used by pedal cycles	Indicate exemptions for buses, taxis and pedal cycles from prohibitions such as turn left ahead and no left turn. These signs may be circular when mounted near traffic signals

Other types of lane

RULE
142 **High-occupancy vehicle lanes and other designated vehicle lanes.** Lanes may be restricted for use by particular types of vehicle; these restrictions may apply some or all of the time. The operating times and vehicle types will be indicated on the accompanying traffic signs. You **MUST NOT** drive in such lanes during their times of operation unless signs indicate that your vehicle is permitted (see Traffic signs).

Vehicles permitted to use designated lanes may or may not include cycles, buses, taxis, licensed private hire vehicles, motorcycles, heavy goods vehicles (HGVs) and high-occupancy vehicles (HOVs).
Where HOV lanes are in operation, they **MUST ONLY** be used by
- vehicles containing at least the minimum number of people indicated on the traffic signs
- any other vehicles, such as buses and motorcycles, as indicated on signs prior to the start of the lane, irrespective of the number of occupants.

Laws RTRA sects 5 & 8, & RTA 1988, sect 36

RULE
143 **One-way streets.** Traffic **MUST** travel in the direction indicated by signs. Buses and/ or cycles may have a contraflow lane. Choose the correct lane for your exit as soon as you can. Do not change lanes suddenly. Unless road signs or markings indicate otherwise, you should use
- the left-hand lane when going left
- the right-hand lane when going right
- the most appropriate lane when going straight ahead.

Remember – traffic could be passing on both sides.

Laws RTA 1988 sect 36 & RTRA sects 5 & 8

City Cycling

Cycling in a city can seem a little intimidating. However, thanks to the ever-increasing provision for cyclists in the planning of road infrastructure and the growing groundswell of public desire to ride bikes in an urban environment, it's becoming safer to ride in many cities.

It is fair to say though that urban riding is very different from countryside riding, requiring a cyclist to focus on a greater number of things at once at any given time.

- **Always be aware of other road users and pedestrians.** Becoming a safe part of a potentially busy stream of traffic, motorised or otherwise, takes a lot of concentration. Do not compromise this awareness by wearing headphones or otherwise reducing sensory feedback. Keep checking to the sides and behind while riding, as well as ahead.
- **Be decisive and assertive** – when deciding to change lane, make a turn or even start off from lights or a junction, do so with as much conviction as possible and make all actions clearly visible to other road users in advance.
- **Be as visible as possible** on the road, day and night, either with bright and reflective clothing, lights or position. Preferably all three.
- **It is better to be a part of the traffic than harassed by the traffic.** A cyclist should ride positioned out from the curb, rather than staying closer to it. The area alongside the curb is filled with drains and leaves little room for emergency manoeuvres, whereas further out it is easier to avoid pedestrians stepping out and the surface is usually better. Most importantly, however, cars are forced to consider the cyclist part of the traffic and are less likely to try and squeeze past. The cyclist should ride confidently and assertively in this position, however.
- **Plan your route** – wherever possible a route should be well researched before departing to avoid tricky last-minute decision-making out on the roads. It can be difficult to follow cycle-route signposts while riding. If a mistake is made, or a wrong lane selected, correct afterwards rather than hesitating.
- **Be cautious when passing or pulling out around parked cars** – traffic behind may not give way to allow passing easily or the driver may open the door unexpectedly. Steer well clear of parked cars. Children may run out from between parked cars.
- **Be extremely careful around trucks, lorries and buses** – these have reduced vision to the rear and sides, which result in blind spots large enough to make even a large group of cyclists invisible to the driver. NEVER pass or pull up alongside a truck or bus on the left.
- **Make eye contact** with drivers nearby at junctions wherever possible, so you can confirm they have seen you.
- **Take security seriously.** See pages 52–53 for advice on parking and security.

TOP TIP After completing a busy route, write down all the hazards you've encountered. Would you tackle any of them differently?

Equipment for urban cycling

- **Good quality and well-charged front and rear lights** if expecting bad weather, poor light conditions or after-dark riding.
- **Bright clothing** or high-visibility accessories such a sash or vest. Reflectives too.
- **Rucksack** – while panniers are definitely convenient, a smallish rucksack can be more stable to ride with or unbalance the bike if only one side is used. Rucksacks can also be adorned with flashing LEDs and reflectives, and are easily taken along with you for security.
- **Smartphone** – mapping software is useful for correcting any route problems, once stationary. Use a smartphone holder on the handlebars.
- **Mudguards** – these keep you dry and avoid fellow cyclists getting road spray in their faces in wet conditions.

Moving and Awareness

The *Highway Code* provides very specific rules for the behaviour of cyclists.

RULE
064 You MUST NOT cycle on a pavement.
Laws HA 1835 sect 72 & R(S)A 1984, sect 129

RULE
066 You should
- keep both hands on the handlebars except when signalling or changing gear
- keep both feet on the pedals
- never ride more than two abreast, and ride in single file on narrow or busy roads and when riding round bends
- not ride close behind another vehicle
- not carry anything which will affect your balance or may get tangled up with your wheels or chain
- be considerate of other road users, particularly blind and partially sighted pedestrians. Let them know you are there when necessary, for example, by ringing your bell if you have one. It is recommended that a bell be fitted.

RULE
067 You should
- look all around before moving away from the kerb, turning or manoeuvring, to make sure it is safe to do so. Give a clear signal to show other road users what you intend to do (see **Arm signals** on page 44)
- look well ahead for obstructions in the road, such as drains, pot-holes and parked vehicles so that you do not have to swerve suddenly to avoid them. Leave plenty of room when passing parked vehicles and watch out for doors being opened or pedestrians stepping into your path
- be aware of traffic coming up behind you
- take extra care near road humps, narrowings and other traffic calming features
- take care when overtaking (see Rules 162–169, pages 48–50).

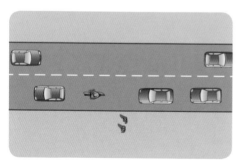

Position yourself where you can both see and be seen. The primary riding position, in the centre of the left-hand lane, is ideal for busy or narrow roads, and when you are riding at the speed of the other traffic.

The secondary riding position, closer to the kerb, will allow you to be overtaken more easily, and is suitable for wide roads and/or low traffic. Keep at least half a metre from the kerb to avoid obstacles in the road.

RULE
068 You MUST NOT
- carry a passenger unless your cycle has been built or adapted to carry one
- hold onto a moving vehicle or trailer
- ride in a dangerous, careless or inconsiderate manner
- ride when under the influence of drink or drugs, including medicine.

Law RTA 1988 sects 24, 26, 28, 29 & 30 as amended by RTA 1991

Moving off: a driver's point of view

General rules 159–160 offer similar advice to those above.

RULE
159 Before moving off you should
- use all mirrors to check the road is clear
- look round to check the blind spots (the areas you are unable to see in the mirrors)
- signal if necessary before moving out
- look round for a final check.

Move off only when it is safe to do so.

Rule 159: Check the blind spot before moving off

Rule 160 advises drivers that, once moving, they should be aware of other road users, especially cycles and motorcycles who may be filtering through the traffic. These are more difficult to see than larger vehicles and their riders are particularly vulnerable. Give them plenty of room, especially if you are driving a long vehicle or towing a trailer.

Signals

The Highway Code's general Rules 103–111 for all road users explain the importance of signals.

RULE
103 Signals warn and inform other road users, including pedestrians, of your intended actions. You should always
- give clear signals in plenty of time, having checked it is not misleading to signal at that time
- use them to advise other road users before changing course or direction, stopping or moving off
- cancel them after use
- make sure your signals will not confuse others. If, for instance, you want to stop after a side road, do not signal until you are passing the road. If you signal earlier it may give the impression that you intend to turn into the road. Your brake lights [if you are a driver] will warn traffic behind you that you are slowing down
- use an arm signal to emphasise or reinforce your signal if necessary. Remember that signalling does not give you priority.

Arm signals

For use by cyclists and those in charge of horses.

I intend to move in to the left or turn left

I intend to move out to the right or turn right

I intend to slow down or stop

Signals by other vehicles

RULE
104 You should also
- watch out for signals given by other road users and proceed only when you are satisfied that it is safe
- be aware that an indicator on another vehicle may not have been cancelled.

RULE
110 Flashing headlights. Only flash your headlights to let other road users know that you are there. Do not flash your headlights to convey any other message or intimidate other road users.

RULE
111 Never assume that flashing headlights is a signal inviting you to proceed. Use your own judgement and proceed carefully.

Direction indicator signals

I intend to move out to the right or turn right   I intend to move in to the left or turn left

Brake light signals

I am applying the brakes   I intend to reverse

These signals should not be used except for the purposes described.

Signals

Signals by authorised persons

RULE
105 You **MUST** obey signals given by police officers, traffic officers, traffic wardens (see below) and signs used by school crossing patrols.
Laws RTRA sect 28, RTA 1988 sect 35, TMA 2004 sect 6, & FTWO art 3

RULE
106 **Police stopping procedures.** If the police want to stop your vehicle they will, where possible, attract your attention by
- flashing blue lights or headlights, or sounding their siren or horn, usually from behind
- directing you to pull over to the side by pointing and/or using the left indicator.
You **MUST** then pull over and stop as soon as it is safe to do so. Then switch off your engine.
Law RTA 1988 sect 163

RULE
107 **Driver and Vehicle Standards Agency Officers** have powers to stop vehicles on all roads, including motorways and trunk roads, in England and Wales. They will attract your attention by flashing amber lights
- either from the front requesting you to follow them to a safe place to stop
- or from behind directing you to pull over to the side by pointing and/or using the left indicator.
It is an offence not to comply with their directions. You **MUST** obey any signals given (see Signals by authorised persons).
Laws RTA 1988, sect 67, & PRA 2002, sect 41 & sched 5(8)

RULE
108 **Traffic Officers** have powers to stop vehicles on most motorways and some 'A' class roads, in England only. If traffic officers in uniform want to stop your vehicle on safety grounds (e.g. an insecure load) they will, where possible, attract your attention by
- flashing amber lights, usually from behind
- directing you to pull over to the side by pointing and/or using the left indicator.
You **MUST** then pull over and stop as soon as it is safe to do so. Then switch off your engine. It is an offence not to comply with their directions (see Signals by authorised persons).
Law RTA 1988, sects 35 & 163 as amended by TMA 2004, sect 6

See page 60–65 and 70–71 for further information on traffic signs and traffic light signals (Rule 109).

Police officers
Stop

Traffic approaching from the front

Traffic approaching from both front and behind

Traffic approaching from behind

To beckon traffic on

From the side

From the front

From behind

School crossing patrols

Not ready to cross pedestrians

Barrier to stop pedestrians crossing

Ready to cross pedestrians, vehicles must be prepared to stop

All vehicles must stop

Overtaking

Rule 67 for cyclists (see page 42) advises cyclists to take care when overtaking.

Rule 67 for cyclists (see page 42)

RULE
162 **Before overtaking** you should make sure
- the road is sufficiently clear ahead
- road users are not beginning to overtake you
- there is a suitable gap in front of the road user you plan to overtake.

RULE
163 **Overtake only** when it is safe and legal to do so. You should
- not get too close to the vehicle you intend to overtake
- use your mirrors [cars and motorcycles], signal when it is safe to do so, take a quick sideways glance if necessary into the blind spot area and then start to move out
- not assume that you can simply follow a vehicle ahead which is overtaking; there may only be enough room for one vehicle
- move quickly past the vehicle you are overtaking, once you have started to overtake. Allow plenty of room. Move back to the left as soon as you can but do not cut in
- take extra care at night and in poor visibility when it is harder to judge speed and distance
- give way to oncoming vehicles before passing parked vehicles or other obstructions on your side of the road
- only overtake on the left if the vehicle in front is signalling to turn right, and there is room to do so
- stay in your lane if traffic is moving slowly in queues. If the queue on your right is moving more slowly than you are, you may pass on the left
- give motorcyclists, cyclists and horse riders at least as much room as you would when overtaking a car (see Rules 211–213 on page 56, and 214–215 on page 57).
Remember: Mirrors [Cyclists: check around you] – Signal – Manoeuvre

Rule 163: Give vulnerable road users at least as much space as you would a car

RULE
164 Large vehicles. Overtaking these is more difficult. You should

- drop back. This will increase your ability to see ahead and should allow the driver of the large vehicle to see you in their mirrors. Getting too close to large vehicles, including agricultural vehicles such as a tractor with a trailer or other fixed equipment, will obscure your view of the road ahead and there may be another slow-moving vehicle in front
- make sure that you have enough room to complete your overtaking manoeuvre before committing yourself. It takes longer to pass a large vehicle. If in doubt do not overtake
- not assume you can follow a vehicle ahead which is overtaking a long vehicle. If a problem develops, they may abort overtaking and pull back in.

Rule 164: Do not cut in too quickly

RULE
165 You **MUST NOT** overtake

- if you would have to cross or straddle double white lines with a solid line nearest to you (but see Rule 129 on page 66)
- if you would have to enter an area designed to divide traffic, if it is surrounded by a solid white line
- the nearest vehicle to a pedestrian crossing, especially when it has stopped to let pedestrians cross
- if you would have to enter a lane reserved for buses, trams or cycles during its hours of operation
- after a 'No Overtaking' sign and until you pass a sign cancelling the restriction.
Laws RTA 1988 sect 36, TSRGD regs 10, 22, 23 & 24, ZPPPCRGD reg 24

RULE
166 DO NOT overtake if there is any doubt, or where you cannot see far enough ahead to be sure it is safe. For example, when you are approaching

- a corner or bend
- a hump bridge
- the brow of a hill.

Overtaking

167 **DO NOT** overtake where you might come into conflict with other road users. For example

- approaching or at a road junction on either side of the road
- where the road narrows
- when approaching a school crossing patrol
- between the kerb and a bus or tram when it is at a stop
- where traffic is queuing at junctions or roadworks
- when you would force another road user to swerve or slow down
- at a level crossing
- when a road user is indicating right, even if you believe the signal should have been cancelled. Do not take a risk; wait for the signal to be cancelled
- stay behind if you are following a cyclist approaching a roundabout or junction, and you intend to turn left
- when a tram is standing at a kerbside tram stop and there is no clearly marked passing lane for other traffic.

RULE

168 **Being overtaken.** If a driver is trying to overtake you, maintain a steady course and speed, slowing down if necessary to let the vehicle pass. Never obstruct drivers who wish to pass. Speeding up or driving unpredictably while someone is overtaking you is dangerous. Drop back to maintain a two-second gap if someone overtakes and pulls into the gap in front of you.

RULE

169 Do not hold up a long queue of traffic, especially if you are driving a large or slow-moving vehicle. Check your mirrors [Cyclists: check around you] frequently, and if necessary, pull in where it is safe and let traffic pass.

Cyclist's Highway Code

Speed Limits

RULE
124 You MUST NOT exceed the maximum speed limits for the road and for your vehicle (see the table below). The presence of street lights generally means that there is a 30mph (48km/h) speed limit unless otherwise specified.
Law RTRA sects 81, 86, 89 & sch 6 (as amended by the MV(VSL)(E&W) regs 2014)

RULE
124 The speed limit is the absolute maximum and does not mean it is safe to drive at that speed irrespective of conditions. Driving at speeds too fast for the road and traffic conditions is dangerous. You should always reduce your speed when
- the road layout or condition presents hazards, such as bends
- sharing the road with pedestrians, cyclists and horse riders, particularly children, and motorcyclists
- weather conditions make it safer to do so
- driving at night as it is more difficult to see other road users.

The right speed

TYPE OF VEHICLE	Built-up areas*	Elsewhere		Motorways**
		Single carriageways	Dual carriageways	
	MPH	MPH	MPH	MPH
Cars & motorcycles (including car derived vans up to 2 tonnes maximum laden weight)	30	60	70	70
Cars towing caravans or trailers (including car derived vans and motorcycles)	30	50	60	60
Buses & coaches (not exceeding 12 metres in overall length)	30	50	60	70
Goods vehicles (not exceeding 7.5 tonnes maximum laden weight)	30	50	60	70†
Goods vehicles (exceeding 7.5 tonnes maximum laden weight)	30	50‡	60§	60

* The 30mph limit usually applies to all traffic on all roads with street lighting unless signs show otherwise.
** Given here for reference. Cyclists must not use motorways (see page 77).
† 50mph if articulated or towing a trailer.
‡ 40mph in Scotland.
§ 50mph in Scotland.

Parking and Security

Rule 70 for cyclists offers advice on security and how to avoid your cycle becoming an obstruction.

RULE
070 When parking your cycle
- find a conspicuous location where it can be seen by passers-by
- use cycle stands or other cycle parking facilities wherever possible
- do not leave it where it would cause an obstruction or hazard to other road users
- secure it well so that it will not fall over and become an obstruction or hazard.

RULE
250 **Parking at night.** Cars, goods vehicles not exceeding 2500kg unladen weight, invalid carriages, motorcycles and pedal cycles may be parked without lights on a road (or lay-by) with a speed limit of 30mph (48km/h) or less if they are
- at least 10 metres (32 feet) away from any junction, close to the kerb and facing in the direction of the traffic flow
- in a recognised parking place or lay-by.

Other vehicles and trailers, and all vehicles with projecting loads, MUST NOT be left on a road at night without lights.
Laws RVLR reg 24 & CUR reg 82(7)

Cycle security

Sadly, bike theft is rife, particularly in urban areas. However, there are a good number of ways in which the risks of bicycle theft can be significantly reduced.

Whenever a bike is left unsupervised during a ride, it is imperative to lock it to something sturdy, preferably a purpose-built bike rack, with a solid and reliable lock. There are many lock types, but they largely fall into the following categories.

- **Shackle Lock** – a u-shaped metal bar with a removable end-section that locks to both ends of the bar.
- **Chain** – a chain that may or may not be covered with a protective coating and that is combined with a padlock.
- **Cable** – an alternative to a chain, usually employing plaited or twisted metal wires instead of chain links.

Each have their own set of problems and advantages, regarding weight and how well they can protect a bicycle from theft. There's a fine balance to be had in finding a lock that isn't too heavy to carry but also is not so light that it doesn't do its job. Some manufacturers have come up with ingenious ways to make riding with a lock easier, such as wearing it around the waist or mounting the lock to the bike when not in use. A guarantee to look out for is the Sold Secure standard, which independently tests locks. Ideally choose a lock marked Sold Secure Silver or Gold.

A shackle lock in use.

Other ways to help deter thieves

- Park the bike somewhere obvious where it can be seen by passers-by.
- Use purpose-built bike parks wherever possible as they are generally more secure and easier to use.
- Make sure that the bike isn't causing an obstruction or is likely to fall over.
- Remove any lights or computers.
- Remove the front wheel and/or saddle if possible and lock securely with the rest of the bike. Use a separate chain as this makes the bike more difficult to ride away.

When parking the bike at home, a ground anchor that the bike can be chained to can be a useful addition to the floor of a locked shed. Also, be wise about security and privacy settings on online communities for fitness and cycling gadgets to prevent accidentally sharing sensitive location information with potential thieves.

Security-marking the bicycle with a kit such as Datatag can, if the worst happens, help police to identify and possibly recover the bike if stolen.

Road Users Requiring Extra Care

Overview

This section of *The Highway Code* is written primarily from the viewpoint of a car driver, but it is still applicable to cyclists.

RULE
204 The most vulnerable road users are pedestrians, cyclists, motorcyclists and horse riders. It is particularly important to be aware of children, older and disabled people, and learner and inexperienced drivers and riders.

Pedestrians

RULE
205 There is a risk of pedestrians, especially children, stepping unexpectedly into the road. You should drive with the safety of children in mind at a speed suitable for the conditions.

RULE
206 **Drive carefully and slowly** when
- in crowded shopping streets, Home Zones and Quiet Lanes or residential areas
- driving past bus and tram stops; pedestrians may emerge suddenly into the road
- passing parked vehicles, especially ice cream vans; children are more interested in ice cream than traffic and may run into the road unexpectedly
- needing to cross a pavement or cycle track; for example, to reach or leave a driveway. Give way to pedestrians and cyclists on the pavement
- reversing into a side road; look all around the vehicle and give way to any pedestrians who may be crossing the road
- turning at road junctions; give way to pedestrians who are already crossing the road into which you are turning
- the pavement is closed due to street repairs and pedestrians are directed to use the road
- approaching pedestrians on narrow rural roads without a footway or footpath. Always slow down and be prepared to stop if necessary, giving them plenty of room as you drive past.

Rule 206: Watch out for children in busy areas

RULE
207 **Particularly vulnerable pedestrians.** These include
- children and older pedestrians who may not be able to judge your speed and could step into the road in front of you.
- older pedestrians who may need more time to cross the road. Be patient and allow them to cross in their own time. Do not hurry them by revving your engine or edging forward
- people with disabilities. People with hearing impairments may not be aware of your vehicle approaching. Those with walking difficulties require more time
- blind or partially sighted people, who may be carrying a white cane or using a guide dog. They may not be able to see you approaching
- deafblind people who may be carrying a white cane with a red band or using a dog with a red and white harness. They may not see or hear instructions or signals.

RULE
208 **Near schools.** Drive slowly and be particularly aware of young cyclists and pedestrians. In some places, there may be a flashing amber signal below the 'School' warning sign which tells you that there may be children crossing the road ahead. Drive very slowly until you are clear of the area.

RULE
209 Drive carefully and slowly when passing a stationary bus showing a 'School Bus' sign as children may be getting on or off.

RULE
210 You **MUST** stop when a school crossing patrol shows a 'Stop for children' sign (see page 47).
Law RTRA sect 28

A 'Stop for children' sign (Rule 210) and a 'School Bus' sign (Rule 209)

Motorcyclists and cyclists: a driver's point of view

**RULE
211** It is often difficult to see motorcyclists and cyclists, especially when they are coming up from behind, coming out of junctions, at roundabouts, overtaking you or filtering through traffic. Always look out for them before you emerge from a junction; they could be approaching faster than you think. When turning right across a line of slow-moving or stationary traffic, look out for cyclists or motorcyclists on the inside of the traffic you are crossing. Be especially careful when turning, and when changing direction or lane. Be sure to check mirrors and blind spots carefully.

*Rule 211: Look out for motorcyclists and cyclists
at junctions*

**RULE
212** When passing motorcyclists and cyclists, give them plenty of room (see Rules 162–167 on pages 48–50). If they look over their shoulder it could mean that they intend to pull out, turn right or change direction. Give them time and space to do so.

**RULE
213** Motorcyclists and cyclists may suddenly need to avoid uneven road surfaces and obstacles such as drain covers or oily, wet or icy patches on the road. Give them plenty of room and pay particular attention to any sudden change of direction they may have to make.

Other road users

RULE
214 **Animals.** When passing animals, drive slowly. Give them plenty of room and be ready to stop. Do not scare animals by sounding your horn, revving your engine or accelerating rapidly once you have passed them. Look out for animals being led, driven or ridden on the road and take extra care. Keep your speed down at bends and on narrow country roads. If a road is blocked by a herd of animals, stop and switch off your engine until they have left the road. Watch out for animals on unfenced roads.

RULE
215 **Horse riders and horse-drawn vehicles.** Be particularly careful of horse riders and horse-drawn vehicles especially when overtaking. Always pass wide and slowly. Horse riders are often children, so take extra care and remember riders may ride in double file when escorting a young or inexperienced horse or rider. Look out for horse riders' and horse drivers' signals and heed a request to slow down or stop. Take great care and treat all horses as a potential hazard; they can be unpredictable, despite the efforts of their rider/driver.

RULE
216 **Older drivers.** Their reactions may be slower than other drivers. Make allowance for this.

RULE
217 **Learners and inexperienced drivers.** They may not be so skilful at anticipating and responding to events. Be particularly patient with learner drivers and young drivers. Drivers who have recently passed their test may display a 'new driver' plate or sticker.

RULE
218 **Home Zones and Quiet Lanes.** These are places where people could be using the whole of the road for a range of activities such as children playing or for a community event. You should drive slowly and carefully and be prepared to stop to allow people extra time to make space for you to pass them in safety.

Rule 218: Home Zone and Quiet Lane signs

Road Users Requiring Extra Care

Other vehicles

RULE
219 Emergency and Incident Support vehicles. You should look and listen for ambulances, fire engines, police, doctors or other emergency vehicles using flashing blue, red or green lights and sirens or flashing headlights, or traffic officer and incident support vehicles using flashing amber lights. When one approaches do not panic. Consider the route of such a vehicle and take appropriate action to let it pass, while complying with all traffic signs. If necessary, pull to the side of the road and stop, but try to avoid stopping before the brow of a hill, a bend or narrow section of road. Do not endanger yourself, other road users or pedestrians and avoid mounting the kerb. Do not brake harshly on approach to a junction or roundabout, as a following vehicle may not have the same view as you.

RULE
220 Powered vehicles used by disabled people. These small vehicles travel at a maximum speed of 8mph (12km/h). On a dual carriageway where the speed limit exceeds 50mph (80km/h) they MUST have a flashing amber beacon, but on other roads you may not have that advance warning.
Law RVLR reg 17(1) & 26

RULE
221 Large vehicles. These may need extra road space to turn or to deal with a hazard that you are not able to see. If you are following a large vehicle, such as a bus or articulated lorry, be aware that the driver may not be able to see you in the mirrors. Be prepared to stop and wait if it needs room or time to turn.

Rule 221: Large vehicles need extra room

RULE
222 Large vehicles can block your view. Your ability to see and to plan ahead will be improved if you pull back to increase your separation distance. Be patient, as larger vehicles are subject to lower speed limits than cars and motorcycles. Many large vehicles may be fitted with speed limiting devices which will restrict speed to 56mph (90km/h) even on a motorway.

Large good vehicles rear markings: Motor vehicles over 7,500 kilograms maximum gross weight and trailers over 3,500 kilograms maximum gross weight.

The vertical markings are also required to be fitted to builders' skips placed in the road, commerical vehicles or combinations longer than 13 metres (optional on combinations between 11 and 13 metres).

RULE
223 **Buses, coaches and trams.** Give priority to these vehicles when you can do so safely, especially when they signal to pull away from stops. Look out for people getting off a bus or tram and crossing the road.

RULE
224 **Electric vehicles.** Be careful of electric vehicles such as milk floats and trams. Trams move quickly but silently and cannot steer to avoid you.

RULE
225 **Vehicles with flashing amber beacons.** These warn of a slow-moving or stationary vehicle (such as a Traffic Officer vehicle, salt spreader, snow plough or recovery vehicle) or abnormal loads, so approach with caution. On unrestricted dual carriageways, motor vehicles first used on or after 1 January 1947 with a maximum speed of 25mph (40km/h) or less (such as tractors) **MUST** use a flashing amber beacon (also see Rule 220).
Law RVLR 1989, reg 17

Signs

The *Highway Code* offers very clear advice for all road users regarding signs.

RULE
069 You MUST obey all traffic signs and traffic light signals.
Laws RTA 1988 sect 36 & TSRGD reg 10(1)

RULE
109 You MUST obey all traffic light signals (see page 70) and traffic signs giving orders, including temporary signals & signs (see pages 61–62). Make sure you know, understand and act on all other traffic and information signs and road markings (see pages 66–69).
Laws RTA 1988 sect 36 & TSRGD regs 10, 15, 16, 25, 26, 27, 28, 29, 36, 38 & 40

The signing system

There are three basic types of traffic sign: signs that give orders, signs that warn and signs that give information. Each type has a different shape. A further guide to the function of a sign is its colour. All triangular signs are red.

Circles give orders

Triangles warn

Rectangles inform

Blue circles generally give a mandatory instruction, such as 'turn left', or indicate a route available only to particular classes of traffic, e.g. buses and cycles only

Red rings or circles tell you what you must not do, e.g. you must not exceed 30mph, no vehicles over the height shown may proceed

Blue rectangles are used for information signs **except** on motorways where blue is used for direction signs

Green rectangles are used for direction signs on primary routes

White rectangles are used for direction signs on non-primary routes, or for plates used in combination with warning and regulatory signs

There are a few exceptions to the shape and colour rules, to give certain signs greater prominence. Examples are the 'STOP' and 'GIVE WAY' signs

Traffic signs

The following signs are commonly in use. A comprehensive explanation of the signing system can be found in the AA book *Know Your Road Signs*, which contains the vast majority of signs a cyclist is likely to encounter. Not all signs are drawn to the same scale. Signs and road markings for cycle routes are on pages 32–39.

Signs giving orders

Signs with red circles are mostly prohibitive. Plates below signs qualify their message.

Entry to 20mph zone

End of 20mph zone

Maximum speed

National speed limit applies

School crossing patrol

Stop and give way

Give way to traffic on major road

No entry for vehicular traffic

Manually operated temporary STOP and GO signs

No vehicles except bicycles being pushed

No cycling

No motor vehicles

No buses (over 8 passenger seats)

No overtaking

No towed caravans

No vehicles carrying explosives

No vehicles or combination of vehicles over length shown

No vehicles over height shown

No vehicles over width shown

Give priority to vehicles from opposite direction

No right turn

No left turn

No goods vehicles over maximum gross weight shown (in tonnes) except for loading and unloading

No vehicles over maximum gross weight shown (in tonnes)

Parking restricted to permit holders

No stopping during period indicated except for buses

No stopping during times shown except for as long as necessary to set down or pick up passengers

No waiting

No stopping (clearway)

Signs with blue circles but no red border mostly give positive instruction.

Ahead only

Turn left ahead (right if symbol reversed)

Turn left (right if symbol reversed)

Keep left (right if symbol reversed)

Vehicles may pass either side to reach same destination

Mini-roundabout (roundabout circulation – give way to vehicles from the immediate right)

Route to be used by pedal cycles only

Segregated pedal cycle and pedestrian route

Minimum speed

End of minimum speed

Buses and cycles only

Trams only

Pedestrian crossing point over tramway

One-way traffic (note: compare circular 'Ahead only' sign

With-flow bus and cycle lane

Contraflow bus lane

With-flow pedal cycle lane

Warning signs
Mostly triangular

Distance to 'STOP' line ahead

Dual carriageway ends

Road narrows on right (left if symbol reversed)

Road narrows on both sides

Distance to 'Give Way' line ahead

Crossroads

Junction on bend ahead

T-junction with priority over vehicles from the right

Staggered junction

Traffic merging from left ahead

Priority through route is indicated by the broader line.

Signs

Double bend first to left (symbol may be reversed)

Roundabout

Uneven road

Plate below some signs

Two-way traffic crosses one-way road

Two-way traffic straight ahead

Opening or swing bridge ahead

Low-flying aircraft or sudden aircraft noise

Falling or fallen rocks

Traffic signals not in use

Traffic signals

Slippery road

Steep hill downwards

Steep hill upwards

(Gradients may be shown as a ratio i.e. 20% = 1:5)

Tunnel ahead

Trams crossing ahead

Level crossing with barrier or gate ahead

Level crossing without barrier or gate ahead

Level crossing without barrier

School crossing patrol ahead (some signs have amber lights which flash when crossings are in use)

Frail (or blind or disabled if shown) pedestrians likely to cross road ahead

Pedestrians in road ahead

Zebra crossing

Overhead electric cable; plate indicates maximum height of vehicles which can pass safely

Available width of
headroom indicated

Sharp deviation of
route to left (or right if
chevrons reversed)

Light signals ahead
at level crossing, airfield
or bridge

Miniature warning lights
at level crossings

Cattle

Wild animals

Wild horses or ponies

Accompanied horses
or ponies

Cycle route ahead

Risk of ice

Traffic queues
likely ahead

Distance over which road
humps extend

Other danger; plate
indicates nature of
danger

Soft verges

Side winds

Hump bridge

Worded warning sign

Quayside or river bank

Risk of grounding

Roadworks ahead

Lines and Lane Markings

Rules 127–132 should be read in conjunction with the diagrams opposite.

Lines and lane markings on the road

RULE
127 **A broken white line.** This marks the centre of the road. When this line lengthens and the gaps shorten, it means that there is a hazard ahead. Do not cross it unless you can see the road is clear and wish to overtake or turn off.

RULE
128 **Double white lines where the line nearest to you is broken.** This means you may cross the lines to overtake if it is safe, provided you can complete the manoeuvre before reaching a solid white line on your side. White direction arrows on the road indicate that you need to get back onto your side of the road.

RULE
129 **Double white lines where the line nearest you is solid.** This means you MUST NOT cross or straddle it unless it is safe and you need to enter adjoining premises or a side road. You may cross the line if necessary, provided the road is clear, to pass a stationary vehicle, or overtake a pedal cycle, horse or road maintenance vehicle, if they are travelling at 10mph (16km/h) or less.
Laws RTA 1988 sect 36 & TSRGD regs 10 & 26

RULE
130 **Areas of white diagonal stripes** or chevrons painted on the road. These are to separate traffic lanes or to protect traffic turning right.
- If the area is bordered by a broken white line, you should not enter the area unless it is necessary and you can see that it is safe to do so.
- If the area is marked with chevrons and bordered by solid white lines you MUST NOT enter it except in an emergency.
Laws MT(E&W)R regs 5, 9, 10 & 16, MT(S)R regs 4, 8, 9 & 14, RTA sect 36 & TSRGD 10(1)

RULE
131 **Lane dividers.** These are short, broken white lines which are used on wide carriageways to divide them into lanes. You should keep between them.

RULE
132 **Reflective road studs** may be used with white lines.
- White studs mark the lanes or the middle of the road.
- Red studs mark the left edge of the road.
- Amber studs mark the central reservation of a dual carriageway or motorway.
- Green studs mark the edge of the main carriageway at lay-bys and slip roads.
- Green/yellow studs indicate temporary adjustments to lane layouts, e.g. where roadworks are taking place.

Across the carriageway

Stop line at signals
or police control

Stop line at 'Stop' sign

Stop line for pedestrians
at a level crossing

Give way to traffic on major
road (can also be used at
mini-roundabouts)

Give way to traffic from the
right at a roundabout

Give way to traffic from the
right at a mini-roundabout

Along the carriageway

Edge line

Centre line
See Rule 127

Hazard warning line
See Rule 127

Double white lines
See Rules 128 and 129

See Rule 130

Lane line
See Rule 131

Lines and Lane Markings

Along the edge of the carriageway

Waiting restrictions

Waiting restrictions indicated by yellow lines apply to the carriageway, pavement and verge. Double yellow lines mean no waiting at any time, unless there are signs that specifically indicate seasonal restrictions. The times at which the restrictions apply for other road markings are shown on nearby plates or on entry signs to controlled parking zones. If no days are shown on the signs, the restrictions are in force every day including Sundays and Bank Holidays.

No waiting at
any time

No waiting during times
shown on sign

Red Route stopping controls

Red lines are used on some roads instead of yellow lines. In London the double and single red lines used on Red Routes indicate that stopping to park, load/unload or to board and alight from a vehicle (except for a licensed taxi or if you hold a Blue Badge) is prohibited. The red lines apply to the carriageway, pavement and verge. The times that the red line prohibitions apply are shown on nearby signs, but the double red line ALWAYS means no stopping at any time.

Red and single yellow lines can only give a guide to the restrictions and controls in force and signs, nearby or at a zone entry, must be consulted.

No stopping at
any time

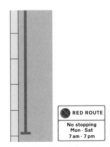

No stopping during
times shown on sign

Other road markings

Keep entrance clear of stationary vehicles, even if picking up or setting down children

Warning of 'Give Way' just ahead

Parking space reserved for vehicles named

Bus stop

Bus lane – see Rule 141 (page 38)

Box junction

Do not block that part of the carriageway indicated

Indication of traffic lanes

Traffic Lights and Waiting

There are two very clear rules in *The Highway Code* regarding traffic lights and it is worth repeating Rule 109 from page 60.

RULE
071 You **MUST NOT** cross the stop line when the traffic lights are red. Some junctions have an advanced stop line to enable you to wait and position yourself ahead of other traffic (see Rule 178, opposite).
Laws RTA 1988 sect 36 & TSRGD regs 10 & 36(1)

RULE
109 You **MUST** obey all traffic light signals and traffic signs giving orders, including temporary signals & signs (see signs on pages 61–65). Make sure you know, understand and act on all other traffic and information signs and road markings (see pages 67–69).
Laws RTA 1988 sect 36 & TSRGD regs 10, 15, 16, 25, 26, 27, 28, 29, 36, 38 & 40

Traffic light signals

RED means 'Stop'. Wait behind the stop line on the carriageway

RED AND AMBER also means 'Stop'. Do not pass through or start until GREEN shows

GREEN means you may go on if the way is clear. Take special care if you intend to turn left or right and give way to pedestrians who are crossing

AMBER means 'Stop' at the stop line. You may go on only if the AMBER appears after you have crossed the stop line or are so close to it that to pull up might cause an accident

A GREEN ARROW may be provided in addition to the full green signal if movement in a certain direction is allowed before or after the full green phase. If the way is clear you may go but only in the direction shown by the arrow. You may do this whatever other lights may be showing. White light signals may be provided for trams.

Signs may be placed with signals to qualify the meaning of the full green signal where movements through a junction are restricted

Light signals for the control of pedal cycles. **RED**, **AMBER** and **GREEN** have the same meaning as at normal traffic signals

Junctions controlled by traffic lights

RULE
175 You **MUST** stop behind the white 'Stop' line across your side of the road unless the light is green. If the amber light appears you may go on only if you have already crossed the stop line or are so close to it that to stop might cause a collision.
Laws RTA 1988 sect 36 & TSRGD regs 10 & 36

RULE
176 You **MUST NOT** move forward over the white line when the red light is showing. Only go forward when the traffic lights are green if there is room for you to clear the junction safely or you are taking up a position to turn right. If the traffic lights are not working, treat the situation as you would an unmarked junction and proceed with great care.
Laws RTA 1988 sect 36 & TSRGD regs 10 & 36

RULE
177 **Green filter arrow.** This indicates a filter lane only. Do not enter that lane unless you want to go in the direction of the arrow. You may proceed in the direction of the green arrow when it, or the full green light shows. Give other traffic, especially cyclists, time and room to move into the correct lane.

RULE
178 **Advanced stop lines.** Some signal-controlled junctions have advanced stop lines to allow cycles to be positioned ahead of other traffic. Motorists, including motorcyclists, **MUST** stop at the first white line reached if the lights are amber or red and should avoid blocking the way or encroaching on the marked area at other times, e.g. if the junction ahead is blocked. If your vehicle has proceeded over the first white line at the time that the signal goes red, you **MUST** stop at the second white line, even if your vehicle is in the marked area. Allow cyclists time and space to move off when the green signal shows.
Laws RTA 1988 sect 36 & TSRGD regs 10, 36(1) & 43(2)

Advanced stop line road marking for pedal cycles at traffic signals.

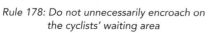
Rule 178: Do not unnecessarily encroach on the cyclists' waiting area

Junctions

Rules 72–75 give cyclists advice on turning at junctions (see pages 73, 75 and 77). Other general rules on road junctions are written from the perspective of a car driver, but apply to all road users.

RULE
170 Take extra care at junctions. You should
- watch out for cyclists, motorcyclists, powered wheelchairs/mobility scooters and pedestrians as they are not always easy to see. Be aware that they may not have seen or heard you if you are approaching from behind
- watch out for pedestrians crossing a road into which you are turning. If they have started to cross they have priority, so give way
- watch out for long vehicles which may be turning at a junction ahead; they may have to use the whole width of the road to make the turn (see Rule 221, page 58)
- watch out for horse riders who may take a different line on the road from that which you would expect
- not assume, when waiting at a junction, that a vehicle coming from the right and signalling left will actually turn. Wait and make sure
- look all around before emerging. Do not cross or join a road until there is a gap large enough for you to do so safely.

Rule 170: Give way to pedestrians who have started to cross

RULE
171 You MUST stop behind the line at a junction with a 'Stop' sign and a solid white line across the road. Wait for a safe gap in the traffic before you move off.
Laws RTA 1988 sect 36 & TSRGD regs 10 & 16

RULE
172 The approach to a junction may have a 'Give Way' sign or a triangle marked on the road. You MUST give way to traffic on the main road when emerging from a junction with broken white lines across the road.
Laws RTA 1988 sect 36 & TSRGD regs 10(1),16(1) & 25

Road junctions on the left

RULE
072 **On the left.** When approaching a junction on the left, watch out for vehicles turning in front of you, out of or into the side road. Just before you turn, check for undertaking cyclists or motorcyclists. Do not ride on the inside of vehicles signalling or slowing down to turn left.

RULE
073 Pay particular attention to long vehicles which need a lot of room to manoeuvre at corners. Be aware that drivers may not see you. They may have to move over to the right before turning left. Wait until they have completed the manoeuvre because the rear wheels come very close to the kerb while turning. Do not be tempted to ride in the space between them and the kerb. (See page 59 for long vehicle markings.)

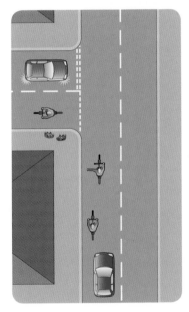

Turning left into a minor road:
Check behind you, then move out into the primary position to prevent vehicles overtaking you and turning across your path.

Check for hazards in the road you are about to turn in to, and watch out for any pedestrians crossing or preparing to cross the road at the head of the junction.

Signal, perform a final check over your left shoulder, and make the turn in the primary position.

Turning left into a major road:
as above, but check for traffic from your right. Be prepared to stop and wait for a gap. Make a final check over your left shoulder before turning.

See also pages 108–110.

Junctions

Turning left – a driver's point of view

Turning left

RULE
182 Use your mirrors and give a left-turn signal well before you turn left. Do not overtake just before you turn left and watch out for traffic coming up on your left before you make the turn, especially if driving a large vehicle. Cyclists, motorcyclists and other road users in particular may be hidden from your view.

Rule 182: Do not cut in on cyclists

RULE
183 When turning
* keep as close to the left as is safe and practicable
* give way to any vehicles using a bus lane, cycle lane or tramway from either direction.

Road junctions on the right

RULE
074 On the right. If you are turning right, check the traffic to ensure it is safe, then signal and move to the centre of the road. Wait until there is a safe gap in the oncoming traffic and give a final look before completing the turn. It may be safer to wait on the left until there is a safe gap or to dismount and push your cycle across the road.

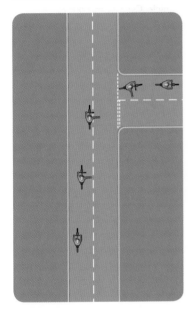

Turning right into a minor road:
Check behind you for a suitable gap in traffic, signal, and then, depending on how wide the road is and how confident you are, move into either the primary position or a position about an arm's length to the left of the centre line.

Continue to signal, perform a final check over your right shoulder and make the turn.

Turning right into a major road:
Observe traffic coming from all sides. Signal as appropriate and be prepared to stop for a gap, ensuring both hands are on the handlebars.

See also pages 108–110.

Turning right – a driver's point of view

Turning right

RULE
179 Well before you turn right you should
- use your mirrors to make sure you know the position and movement of traffic behind you
- give a right-turn signal
- take up a position just left of the middle of the road or in the space marked for traffic turning right
- leave room for other vehicles to pass on the left, if possible.

Junctions

RULE
180 Wait until there is a safe gap between you and any oncoming vehicle. Watch out for cyclists, motorcyclists, pedestrians and other road users. Check your mirrors and blind spot again to make sure you are not being overtaken, then make the turn. Do not cut the corner. Take great care when turning into a main road; you will need to watch for traffic in both directions and wait for a safe gap.
Remember: Mirrors – Signal – Manoeuvre

RULE
181 When turning right at crossroads where an oncoming vehicle is also turning right, there is a choice of two methods
  • turn right side to right side; keep the other vehicle on your right and turn behind it. This is generally the safer method as you have a clear view of any approaching traffic when completing your turn
  • left side to left side, turning in front of each other. This can block your view of oncoming vehicles, so take extra care. Cyclists and motorcyclists in particular may be hidden from your view. Road layout, markings or how the other vehicle is positioned can determine which course should be taken.

Box junctions

RULE
174 These have criss-cross yellow lines painted on the road (see Road markings on page 69). You **MUST NOT** enter the box until your exit road or lane is clear. However, you may enter the box and wait when you want to turn right, and are only stopped from doing so by oncoming traffic, or by other vehicles waiting to turn right. At signalled roundabouts you **MUST NOT** enter the box unless you can cross over it completely without stopping.
Law TSRGD regs 10(1) & 29(2)

Rule 174: Enter a box junction only if your exit road is clear

Multi-lane Roads

Lane discipline

RULE
133 If you need to change lane, first use your mirrors [cyclists: look around you] and if necessary take a quick sideways glance to make sure you will not force another road user to change course or speed. When it is safe to do so, signal to indicate your intentions to other road users and when clear, move over.

RULE
134 You should follow the signs and road markings and get into the lane as directed. In congested road conditions do not change lanes unnecessarily. Merging in turn is recommended but only if safe and appropriate when vehicles are travelling at a very low speed, e.g. when approaching roadworks. It is not recommended at high speed.

RULE
135 Where a single carriageway has three lanes and the road markings or signs do not give priority to traffic in either direction
- use the middle lane only for overtaking or turning right. Remember, you have no more right to use the middle lane than a driver coming from the opposite direction
- do not use the right-hand lane.

RULE
136 Where a single carriageway has four or more lanes, use only the lanes that signs or markings indicate.

Dual carriageways
A dual carriageway is a road which has a central reservation to separate the carriageways. Rule 75 is a featured rule for cyclists.

RULE
137 On a two-lane dual carriageway you should stay in the left-hand lane. Use the right-hand lane for overtaking or turning right. After overtaking, move back to the left-hand lane when it is safe to do so.

RULE
138 On a three-lane dual carriageway, you may use the middle lane or the right-hand lane to overtake but return to the middle and then the left-hand lane when it is safe.

RULE
075 Remember that traffic on most dual carriageways moves quickly. When crossing wait for a safe gap and cross each carriageway in turn. Take extra care when crossing slip roads.

Motorways
Rule 253 says that 'Motorways **MUST NOT** be used by cyclists'.

Roundabouts

Roundabouts can be very intimidating for all levels of riders.

RULE
076 Full details about the correct procedure at roundabouts are contained in Rules 184–190 (see below, and pages 79–81). Roundabouts can be hazardous and should be approached with care.

RULE
077 You may feel safer walking your cycle round on the pavement or verge. If you decide to ride round keeping to the left-hand lane you should
- be aware that drivers may not easily see you
- take extra care when cycling across exits. You may need to signal right to show you are not leaving the roundabout
- watch out for vehicles crossing your path to leave or join the roundabout.

RULE
078 Give plenty of room to long vehicles on the roundabout as they need more space to manoeuvre. Do not ride in the space they need to get round the roundabout. It may be safer to wait until they have cleared the roundabout.

RULE
184 **On approaching a roundabout** take notice and act on all the information available to you, including traffic signs, traffic lights and lane markings which direct you into the correct lane. You should
- use Mirrors [Cyclists: check around you] – Signal – Manoeuvre at all stages
- decide as early as possible which exit you need to take
- give an appropriate signal (see Rule 186, page 180). Time your signals so as not to confuse other road users
- get into the correct lane
- adjust your speed and position to fit in with traffic conditions
- be aware of the speed and position of all the road users around you.

RULE
185 When reaching the roundabout you should

- give priority to traffic approaching from your right, unless directed otherwise by signs, road markings or traffic lights
- check whether road markings allow you to enter the roundabout without giving way. If so, proceed, but still look to the right before joining
- watch out for all other road users already on the roundabout; be aware they may not be signalling correctly or at all
- look forward before moving off to make sure traffic in front has moved off.

Rule 185: Follow the correct procedure at roundabouts

Roundabouts

RULE

186 **Signals and position.** When taking the first exit, unless signs or markings indicate otherwise
- signal left and approach in the left-hand lane
- keep to the left on the roundabout and continue signalling left to leave.

When taking an exit to the right or going full circle, unless signs or markings indicate otherwise
- signal right and approach in the right-hand lane
- keep to the right on the roundabout until you need to change lanes to exit the roundabout
- signal left after you have passed the exit before the one you want.

When taking any intermediate exit, unless signs or markings indicate otherwise
- select the appropriate lane on approach to and on the roundabout
- you should not normally need to signal on approach
- stay in this lane until you need to alter course to exit the roundabout
- signal left after you have passed the exit before the one you want.

When there are more than three lanes at the entrance to a roundabout, use the most appropriate lane on approach and through it.

Signals and position at roundabouts: The blue rider is taking the first exit, the red rider is taking the right exit and the green rider is going straight ahead.

RULE
187 In all cases watch out for and give plenty of room to
- pedestrians who may be crossing the approach and exit roads
- traffic crossing in front of you on the roundabout, especially vehicles intending to leave by the next exit
- traffic which may be straddling lanes or positioned incorrectly
- motorcyclists
- cyclists and horse riders who may stay in the left-hand lane and signal right if they intend to continue round the roundabout. Allow them to do so
- long vehicles (including those towing trailers). These might have to take a different course or straddle lanes either approaching or on the roundabout because of their length. Watch out for their signals.

RULE
188 **Mini-roundabouts.** Approach these in the same way as normal roundabouts. All vehicles MUST pass round the central markings except large vehicles which are physically incapable of doing so. Remember, there is less space to manoeuvre and less time to signal. Avoid making U-turns at mini-roundabouts. Beware of others doing this.
Laws RTA 1988 sect 36 & TSRGD regs 10(1) & 16(1)

A mini-roundabout is normally found on a road with a speed limit of 30mph (48 km/h) or less. It should be treated the same as a conventional roundabout. You must give way to traffic from the right, and keep to the left of the white circle.

RULE
189 At double mini-roundabouts treat each roundabout separately and give way to traffic from the right.

RULE
190 **Multiple roundabouts.** At some complex junctions, there may be a series of mini-roundabouts at each intersection. Treat each mini-roundabout separately and follow the normal rules.

Crossing the Road

The Highway Code offers the following advice to cyclists when crossing a road.

RULE
079 Do not ride across equestrian crossings, as they are for horse riders only. Do not ride across a pelican, puffin or zebra crossing (see pages 84–86). Dismount and wheel your cycle across.

RULE
080 **Toucan crossings.** These are light-controlled crossings which allow cyclists and pedestrians to share crossing space and cross at the same time. They are push-button operated. Pedestrians and cyclists will see the green signal together. Cyclists are permitted to ride across.

Rule 80: Toucan crossings can be used by both cyclists and pedestrians

RULE
081 **Cycle-only crossings.** Cycle tracks (see pages 32–33) on opposite sides of the road may be linked by signalled crossings. You may ride across but you MUST NOT cross until the green cycle symbol is showing.
Law TSRGD regs 33(2) & 36(1)

Toucan crossings

Cyclists may ride across toucans, whereas they should dismount at other crossings (see Rules 79 and 80, opposite).

A toucan crossing is used by both pedestrians and cyclists. Pedestrian and cycle signals are side by side and may be either near-side signals as for puffin crossings, or located on the opposite side of the road (far-side signals). The signals for traffic travelling along the road (including cycles) operate in the same manner as those for puffin crossings (see Rule 199 on page 86 and the light signals on page 70).

Cyclists who need to cross the road will be directed to a cycle facility off the main carriageway, adjacent to the waiting area for pedestrians. Near-side signals include red and green pedal cycle symbols, together with a call button for use by both pedestrians and cyclists (see below).

The far-side crossing signals have both the green and red pedestrian signals, but only a green cycle signal. If the red standing figure is showing, either a pedestrian or cyclist should push the call button and wait until the green pedestrian and cycle signals show.

Near-side signals for toucan crossing

Far-side signals for toucan crossing

Crossings

Pages 82–83 look at how and where cyclists should cross a road. The following rules deal with how vehicles and cyclists should approach different types of crossing while on the road.

Pedestrian crossings

RULE
191 You MUST NOT park on a crossing or in the area covered by the zig-zag lines. You MUST NOT overtake the moving vehicle nearest the crossing or the vehicle nearest the crossing which has stopped to give way to pedestrians.
Laws ZPPPCRGD regs 18, 20 & 24, RTRA sect 25(5) & TSRGD regs 10, 27 & 28

RULE
192 In queuing traffic, you should keep the crossing clear.

Rule 192: Keep the crossing clear

RULE
193 You should take extra care where the view of either side of the crossing is blocked by queuing traffic or incorrectly parked vehicles. Pedestrians may be crossing between stationary vehicles.

RULE
194 Allow pedestrians plenty of time to cross and do not harass them by revving your engine [drivers] or edging forward.

RULE
195 **Zebra crossings.** As you approach a zebra crossing
- look out for pedestrians waiting to cross and be ready to slow down or stop to let them cross
- you **MUST** give way when a pedestrian has moved onto a crossing
- allow more time for stopping on wet or icy roads
- do not wave or use your horn to invite pedestrians across; this could be dangerous if another vehicle is approaching
- be aware of pedestrians approaching from the side of the crossing.

A zebra crossing with a central island is two separate crossings.
Law ZPPPCRGD reg 25

Zebra crossings have flashing beacons

Zebra crossings with a central island are two separate crossings

Crossings

Signal-controlled crossings

RULE
196 **Pelican crossings.** These are signal-controlled crossings where flashing amber follows the red 'Stop' light. You MUST stop when the red light shows. When the amber light is flashing, you MUST give way to any pedestrians on the crossing. If the amber light is flashing and there are no pedestrians on the crossing, you may proceed with caution.
Laws ZPPPCRGD regs 23 & 26 & RTRA sect 25(5)

Rule 196: Allow pedestrians to cross when the amber light is flashing

RULE
197 Pelican crossings which go straight across the road are one crossing, even when there is a central island. You MUST wait for pedestrians who are crossing from the other side of the island.
Laws ZPPPCRGD reg 26 & RTRA sect 25(5)

RULE
198 Give way to anyone still crossing after the signal for vehicles has changed to green. This advice applies to all crossings.

RULE
199 **Toucan, puffin and equestrian crossings.** These are similar to pelican crossings, but there is no flashing amber phase; the light sequence for traffic at these three crossings is the same as at traffic lights (see page 70). If the signal-controlled crossing is not working, proceed with extreme caution.

Level crossings

Read the following rules alongside pages 70–71 (rules 71 and 109), which provide very clear guidance on obeying lights.

RULE 082 **Level crossings/Tramways.** Take extra care when crossing the tracks (see Rule 306 below). You should dismount at level crossings where a 'cyclist dismount' sign is displayed.

RULE 306 All road users, but particularly cyclists and motorcyclists, should take extra care when driving or riding close to or crossing the tracks, especially if the rails are wet. You should take particular care when crossing the rails at shallow angles, on bends and at junctions. It is safest to cross the tracks directly at right angles. Other road users should be aware that cyclists and motorcyclists may need more space to cross the tracks safely.

RULE 291 A level crossing is where a road crosses a railway or tramway line. Approach and cross it with care. Never drive onto a crossing until the road is clear on the other side and do not get too close to the car in front. Never stop or park on, or near a crossing.

RULE 292 **Overhead electric lines.** It is dangerous to touch overhead electric lines. You MUST obey the safe height warning road signs and you should not continue forward onto the railway if your vehicle touches any height barrier or bells. The clearance available is usually 5 metres (16 feet 6 inches) but may be lower.
Laws RTA 1988 sect 36, TSRGD 2002 reg 17(5)

Rule 293: Stop when the traffic lights show

Crossings

RULE
293 **Controlled Crossings.** Most crossings have traffic light signals with a steady amber light, twin flashing red stop lights (see below) and an audible alarm for pedestrians. They may have full, half or no barriers.

* You **MUST** always obey the flashing red stop lights.
* You **MUST** stop behind the white line across the road.
* Keep going if you have already crossed the white line when the amber light comes on.
* Do not reverse onto or over a controlled crossing.
* You **MUST** wait if a train goes by and the red lights continue to flash. This means another train will be passing soon.
* Only cross when the lights go off and barriers open.
* Never zig-zag around half-barriers, they lower automatically because a train is approaching.
* At crossings where there are no barriers, a train is approaching when the lights show.

Laws RTA 1988 sect 36 & TSRGD regs 10 & 40

Road traffic signals at a level crossing.

Automatic open level crossings have flashing signals and audible warnings. The lights will flash and the warnings will sound until it is safe to cross.

Open level crossings without gates, barriers or road traffic light signals have 'give way' signs over a symbol of a railway locomotive.

Alternatively flashing red lights mean you must stop. In addition to level crossings, these signals may be used at other locations, such as lifting bridges, airfields or fire stations. When the **RED** lights are flashing you must stop. **AMBER** has the same meaning as at normal traffic signals.

The St Andrew's cross is used at level crossings where there are no gates or barriers (see above centre and right). At automatic crossings, you must always **STOP** when the traffic light signals show. At crossings with 'Give Way' signs, always look out for and give way to trains.

RULE
294 **Railway telephones.** If you are driving a large or slow-moving vehicle, a long, low vehicle with a risk of grounding, or herding animals, a train could arrive before you are clear of the crossing. You MUST obey any sign instructing you to use the railway telephone to obtain permission to cross. You MUST also telephone when clear of the crossing if requested to do so.
Laws RTA 1988 sect 36 & TSRGD regs 10 & 16(1)

RULE
295 **Crossings without traffic lights.** Vehicles should stop and wait at the barrier or gate when it begins to close and not cross until the barrier or gate opens.

RULE
296 **User-operated gates or barriers.** Some crossings have 'Stop' signs and small red and green lights. You MUST NOT cross when the red light is showing, only cross if the green light is on. If crossing with a vehicle, you should
- open the gates or barriers on both sides of the crossing
- check that the green light is still on and cross quickly
- close the gates or barriers when you are clear of the crossing.
Laws RTA 1988 sect 36 & TSRGD regs 10 & 52(2)

RULE
297 If there are no lights, follow the procedure in Rule 295. Stop, look both ways and listen before you cross. If there is a railway telephone, always use it to contact the signal operator to make sure it is safe to cross. Inform the signal operator again when you are clear of the crossing.

RULE
298 **Open crossings.** These have no gates, barriers, attendant or traffic lights but will have a 'Give Way' sign. You should look both ways, listen and make sure there is no train coming before you cross.

RULE
299 **Incidents and breakdowns.** If your vehicle breaks down, or if you have an incident on a crossing you should
- get everyone out of the vehicle and clear of the crossing immediately
- use a railway telephone if available to tell the signal operator. Follow the instructions you are given
- move the vehicle clear of the crossing if there is time before a train arrives. If the alarm sounds, or the amber light comes on, leave the vehicle and get clear of the crossing immediately.

Tramways

See also rule 306, under Level Crossings on page 87.

RULE
300 You MUST NOT enter a road, lane or other route reserved for trams. Take extra care where trams run along the road. You should avoid driving directly on top of the rails and should take care where trams leave the main carriageway to enter the reserved route, to ensure you do not follow them. The width taken up by trams is often shown by tram lanes marked by white lines, yellow dots or by a different type of road surface. Diamond-shaped signs and white light signals give instructions to tram drivers only.
Law RTRA sects 5 & 8

RULE
301 Take extra care where the track crosses from one side of the road to the other and where the road narrows and the tracks come close to the kerb. Tram drivers usually have their own traffic signals and may be permitted to move when you are not. Always give way to trams. Do not try to race or overtake them or pass them on the inside, unless they are at tram stops or stopped by tram signals and there is a designated tram lane for you to pass.

RULE
302 You MUST NOT park your vehicle where it would get in the way of trams or where it would force other drivers to do so. Do not stop on any part of a tram track, except in a designated bay where this has been provided alongside and clear of the track. When doing so, ensure that all parts of your vehicle are outside the delineated tram path. Remember that a tram cannot steer round an obstruction.
Law RTRA sects 5 & 8

RULE
303 **Tram stops.** Where the tram stops at a platform, either in the middle or at the side of the road, you MUST follow the route shown by the road signs and markings. At stops without platforms you MUST NOT drive between a tram and the left-hand kerb when a tram has stopped to pick up passengers. If there is no alternative route signed, do not overtake the tram – wait until it moves off.
Law RTRA sects 5 & 8

RULE
304 Look out for pedestrians, especially children, running to catch a tram approaching a stop.

RULE
305 Always give priority to trams, especially when they signal to pull away from stops, unless it would be unsafe to do so. Remember that they may be carrying large numbers of standing passengers who could be injured if the tram had to make an emergency stop. Look out for people getting off a bus or tram and crossing the road.

Trams can run on roads used by other vehicles and pedestrians. The part of the road used by trams (the 'swept path') may have a different colour or textured surface to the rest of the road, or it may be edged with special road markings. **Keep the 'swept path' clear.** Trams cannot move out of the way of other road users!

Route for trams only (and buses where the upper sign also includes the bus symbol)

Indication of a tram-only route at a junction ahead

Warning of trams crossing the road ahead

Road marking indicating the start of a route for trams only (and buses when varied to 'TRAM & BUS ONLY')

Reminder to pedestrians to look out for trams approaching from both directions

Drivers of other vehicles must give way to trams at level crossings without barriers, gates or road traffic light signals. Sometimes just a 'Give Way' sign and a tram plate may be used

Incidents and Obstructions

Rule 279 says that if anything falls [from your cycle or another vehicle] on to the road, stop and retrieve it only if it is safe to do so.

RULE
281 **Warning signs or flashing lights.** If you see or hear emergency or incident support vehicles in the distance, be aware there may be an incident ahead (see Rule 219 on page 58). Police officers and traffic officers may be required to work in the carriageway, for example dealing with debris, collisions or conducting rolling road blocks. Police officers will use rear-facing flashing red and blue lights and traffic officers will use rear-facing flashing red and amber lights in these situations. Watch out for such signals, slow down and be prepared to stop. You **MUST** follow any directions given by police officers or traffic officers as to whether you can safely pass the incident or blockage.
Laws RTA1988, sects 35 & 163, and as amended by TMA 2004, sect 6

RULE
282 When passing the scene of an incident or crash do not be distracted or slow down unnecessarily (for example if an incident is on the other side of a dual carriageway). This may cause a collision or traffic congestion, but see summary of Rule 283 below.

Rule 283 says that if you are involved in a crash or stop to give assistance
- ask drivers to switch off their engines and stop smoking
- arrange for the emergency services to be called immediately with full details of the incident location and any casualties
- move uninjured people away from the vehicles to safety
- do not move injured people from their vehicles unless they are in immediate danger from fire or explosion
- do not remove a motorcyclist's helmet unless it is essential to do so
- be prepared to give first aid (see pages 94–95)
- stay at the scene until emergency services arrive.

Incidents involving dangerous goods

RULE
284 Vehicles carrying dangerous goods in packages will be marked with plain orange reflective plates. Road tankers and vehicles carrying tank containers of dangerous goods will have hazard warning plates.

This panel will be displayed by vehicles carrying certain dangerous goods in packages.

The panel illustrated is for flammable liquid. Diamond symbols indicating other risks may be present.

RULE
285 If an incident involves a vehicle containing dangerous goods, follow the advice in Rule 283 and, in particular
- switch off engines and **DO NOT SMOKE**
- keep well away from the vehicle and do not be tempted to try to rescue casualties as you yourself could become one
- call the emergency services and give as much information as possible about the labels and markings on the vehicle. **DO NOT** use a mobile phone close to a vehicle carrying flammable loads.

Documentation

RULE
286 If you are involved in a collision which causes damage or injury to any other person, vehicle, animal or property, you **MUST**
- stop
- give your own and the vehicle owner's name and address, and the registration number of the vehicle, to anyone having reasonable grounds for requiring them
- if you do not give your name and address at the time of the collision, report it to the police as soon as reasonably practicable, and in any case within 24 hours.
Law RTA 1988 sect 170

Roadworks

RULE
288 When the 'Road Works Ahead' sign is displayed, you will need to be more watchful and look for additional signs providing more specific instructions. Observe all signs – they are there for your safety and the safety of road workers.
- You **MUST NOT** exceed any temporary maximum speed limit.
- Use your mirrors and get into the correct lane for your vehicle in good time and as signs direct.
- Do not switch lanes to overtake queuing traffic.
- Take extra care near cyclists and motorcyclists as they are vulnerable to skidding on grit, mud or other debris at roadworks.
- Where lanes are restricted due to roadworks, merge in turn.
- Do not drive through an area marked off by traffic cones.
- Watch out for traffic entering or leaving the works area, but do not be distracted by what is going on there. Concentrate on the road ahead, not the roadworks.
- Bear in mind that the road ahead may be obstructed by the works or by slow moving or stationary traffic.
- Keep a safe distance – there could be queues in front.
Law RTRA sect 16

First Aid on the Road

The following information, from Annexe 7 of *The Highway Code*, may be of general assistance, but there's no substitute for proper training. Any first aid given at the scene of an incident should be looked on only as a temporary measure until the emergency services arrive. If you haven't had any first aid training, the following points could be helpful.

1. Deal with danger

Further collisions and fire are the main dangers following a crash. Approach any vehicle involved with care. Switch off all engines and, if possible, warn other traffic. Stop anyone from smoking.

2. Get help

Try to get the assistance of bystanders. Get someone to call the appropriate emergency services on 999 or 112 as soon as possible. They will need to know the exact location of the incident and the number of vehicles involved. Try to give information about the condition of any casualties, e.g. if anyone is having difficulty breathing, is bleeding heavily or does not respond when spoken to.

3. Help those involved

DO NOT move casualties still in vehicles unless there is the threat of further danger. **DO NOT** remove a motorcyclist's helmet unless it is essential. Remember the casualty may be suffering from shock. **DO NOT** give them anything to eat or drink.

DO try to make them warm and as comfortable as you can. Protect them from rain or snow, but avoid unnecessary movement. **DO** give reassurance confidently and try not to leave them alone or let them wander into the path of other traffic.

4. Provide emergency care

Remember the letters **D R A B C**:

D Danger Check that you are not in danger.

R Response Try to get a response by asking questions and gently shaking their shoulders.

A Airway If the person is not talking and the airway may be blocked, then place one hand under the chin and lift the chin up and forwards. If they are still having difficulty with breathing, then gently tilt the head back.

B Breathing Normal breathing should be established. Once the airway is open check breathing for up to ten seconds.

C Compressions If they have no signs of life and there is no pulse, then chest compressions should be administered. Place two hands in the centre of the chest and press down hard and fast – 5–6cm and about twice a second. You may only need one hand for a child and shouldn't press down as far. For infants, use two fingers in the middle of the chest when delivering compressions and don't press down too far.

If the casualty is unconscious and breathing, place them in the recovery position until medical help arrives

Bleeding. First, check for anything that may be in the wound, such as glass. Taking care not to press on the object, build up padding on either side of the object. If there's nothing embedded, apply firm pressure over the wound to stem the flow of blood. As soon as practical, fasten a pad to the wound with a bandage or length of cloth. Use the cleanest material available. If a limb is bleeding but not broken, raise it above the level of the heart to reduce the flow of blood. Any restriction of blood circulation for more than a short time could cause long-term injuries.

Burns. Check the casualty for shock, and if possible, try to cool the burn for at least ten minutes with plenty of clean, cold water or other non-toxic liquid. Don't try to remove anything that's sticking to the burn.

5. Be prepared

Always carry a first aid kit – you might never need it, but it could save a life. Learn first aid – you can get first-aid training from a qualified organisation such as St John Ambulance, St Andrew's First Aid, British Red Cross or any suitable qualified body (see Useful Contacts on page 128).

Learning to Ride

The National Standard for Cycle Training is designed to help children gain practical cycling skills and feel confident cycling on the road. It is divided into three levels, to take trainees from basic beginner's skills to being able to plan and make an independent journey on busier roads, alongside traffic.

- **Level 1** involves mastery and control of the bicycle in off-road settings and prepares trainees for on-road cycling.
- **Level 2** involves cycling on quieter roads and simple junctions, and covers effective road positioning, communication with other road users and rights of way.
- **Level 3** involves cycling on busier roads and more complex junctions, including hazard awareness and risk management on all roads where cycling is permitted.

Bikeability skills

The National Standard is promoted through Bikeability and is delivered by registered providers, usually in small groups and in many schools between Years 5 and 7. It's a practical participation course rather than a pass/fail course. To find a Bikeability course near you, visit www.bikeability.org.uk

To get the most out of your training, you should:
- work at each practical skill until you can demonstrate it competently, confidently and consistently
- be able to explain why you are performing (or not performing) each action
- not be afraid to ask an instructor to repeat a demonstration
- expect trainers to provide you with feedback so you know where to improve.

Most importantly, take your time practising until you feel safe, comfortable and confident with your riding. Where relevant, each exercise in this section will connect you with the rules of *The Highway Code* (see pages 26–95) and help supplement the practical skills you'll learn with Bikeability.

Bikeability covers the skills cyclists need to know. This section is a companion to the three levels of the National Standard.

Learning to Ride

National Standard for Cycle Training – Level 1

1 Demonstrate an understanding of safety equipment and clothing

Think about how your choice of clothing for riding. Look at the picture below and list at least two things the rider could do to help him be better seen by other road users.

Answers

1 ....

2 ....

Hint: *Clothing and equipment must be fitted and worn correctly. The rider could wear reflective clothing to help him be more visible to other road users. In addition, he could wear lighter-coloured clothing and fit reflectors to the bike. Read* **RULE 059** *(page 28) to understand how a choice of clothing may have an impact on your cycling.*

2 Carry out a simple bike check

Which parts of your bike should you check are in working order before a ride? Indicate where they are on the picture below.

Hint: *You should be able to spot simple faults in your bike's brakes, tyres, wheels, steering and chain, even if you don't know how to fix them. Remember, you must have working brakes by law, and use lights if you're riding at night – see* **ANNEXE 1** *(page 27) for more details.*

3 Get on and off the bike without help

Practise getting on and off your bike in a controlled manner. Do you know which side of the bike you should mount from?

TOP TIP

PARENTS:
If your child is having trouble getting on and off their bike then it's possible that it is the wrong size for them; consult the sizing chart on page 9 as a starting point.

Answer ....

Hint: Applying the brakes whilst mounting and dismounting will help to hold the bike steady. Traffic when riding will usually be on your right-hand side, so it's safest to mount and dismount on the left.

4 Start off and pedal without help

Practise starting off and pedalling while remaining in control of the bike. Look at the diagrams below and indicate which is the 'pedal-ready' position?

✘ or ✔

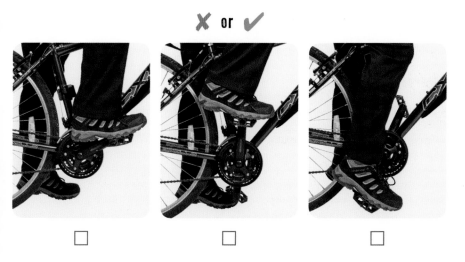

☐   ☐   ☐

Hint: Keeping one foot on the ground, and using your brakes, will help to keep your bike stable while you prepare to move off. The 'pedal-ready' position, with the pedal roughly at 2 o'clock, is the most effective way to move off quickly and with control. Make sure to keep both feet on the pedals as you move, using the balls of your feet, and look where you're going!

National Standard for Cycle Training – Level 1

5 Stop without help

Practise coming to a controlled stop, without using your feet on the ground. Can you list two reasons why it's important to use both brakes at the same time?

Answers

1 ....
2 ....

Hint: You should be able to use both brakes effectively to slow down and stop, then put a foot down on the ground. Be aware that using just the front brake could cause you to fly over the handlebars, and using just the rear one could result in a rear-wheel skid.

6 & 7 Ride along without help for roughly one minute or more; make the bike go where you want

Practise until you can ride and steer comfortably, whilst looking ahead, without wobbling.

Hint: Be sure to keep hold of your brakes in case you lose control or need to stop suddenly. If you are going to cycle on the road, make sure you've read RULE 066 and RULE 067 of the Highway Code (page 42) before you do so.

8 Use gears (where present)

If your bike has gears, you should know how to use them correctly.

When should you use a low gear?

Answer ....

When should you use a high gear?

Answer ....

Hint: How to use the gears on your bike will depend on the type that it is fitted with (see page 10). As a rule, you should start off in a low gear and then move up into a higher one. Low gears will make pedalling easier if you're pedalling uphill or into the wind; higher gears are better on the flat and downhill.

9 Stop quickly with control

Practise making an 'emergency stop', without putting your feet down.

Hint: *You should brace your arms to prevent yourself being thrown forwards.*

10 Manoeuvre safely to avoid objects

Practise manoeuvring around objects at different speeds. Think about how going at different speeds affects your control of the bike.

Hint: *Moving at a lower speed requires greater balance, so can be a difficult skill to learn. When you ride on the road you will likely encounter drains, potholes and parked vehicles, as well as pedestrians. See* **RULE 067** *of the Highway Code (page 42).*

11 Look all around, including behind, without loss of control

Practise looking behind you, over both shoulders, whilst riding in a straight line. Ask a parent or friend to help you practise your observation skills by setting things up behind you for you to spot.

Hint: *Being able look behind you without losing control of the bike is an important skill, and mastering it will help you later on in your cycle training.* **RULE 067** *(page 42) reminds you to be aware of traffic coming up behind you on the road, which is one place where you'll need to put this into practice.*

12 Control the bike with one hand

Practise riding along using just one hand, ensuring that you can remain in control using both the right and the left hand. Think about times when you might need to have just one hand on the handlebars, and when it's important to use both.

Hint: *Having the balance and control to ride a bike using just one hand is important for when you come to learn signalling. Remember, though, that you should still have both hands on the handlebars when turning and stopping (see* **RULE 066**, *page 42).*

National Standard for Cycle Training – Level 1

LEVEL 1 (OPTIONAL)

The following skills are non-compulsory sections of the National Standard for Cycle Training, but it is recommended that all trainee riders ensure that they have an understanding of the theory and techniques outlined here.

13 Share space with pedestrians and other cyclists

Practise cycling in places with both pedestrians and other cyclists, approaching them from the same direction, the opposite direction, or crossing their path.

What hazards might you need to look out for?

Answers

1
2
3

How should you signal your presence and intentions to others?

Answers

1
2

Hint: *It's important that you cycle considerately in areas where other pedestrians or cyclists are present. You should slow your speed and make your presence known – it is recommended that your bike is fitted with a bell. Don't pass too close or too quickly, and if space is limited then wait your turn.*

Be aware that other cyclists and pedestrians may hesitate, stop, or change their direction suddenly. You can avoid collisions by making sure to keep your distance, and keeping your speed under control. See **RULES 067–068** *(pages 42–43) for the Highway Code specifications for cyclists.*

National Standard for Cycle Training – Level 2

1 Demonstrate knowledge of Level 1 (see pages 98–102)

2 Start an on-road journey

Consider where the safest place on the road to start your journey from would be. Can you list three things that you should look out for before pulling away?

Answers

1

2

3

Hint: *You must always start your on-road journey from a position where you can both see and be seen – normally by the kerb, unless parked cars are obscuring the visibility, when you should start outside them. Check for traffic approaching you from behind, approaching vehicles that may turn across your path, and pedestrians that may step out in front of you. Wait for a suitable gap in the traffic before setting off, in a clear and assertive manner (**RULE 067**, page 42).*

TOP TIP
RULE 159 of the Highway Code (page 43) gives instructions for drivers when setting off – you should be aware of these rules, and adapt them to a cyclist as appropriate.

3 Finish an on-road journey

Think about how you would stop safely when riding in traffic. List three things that you should do, in order, before coming to a complete stop.

Answers

1

2

3

Hint: *Before coming to a stop, you must check that it is safe to do so. Check over your shoulder for close following traffic, particularly any vehicles that might be about to overtake or undertake. Do your best to make eye contact with anyone following you, and signal if appropriate (page 44 indicates the arm signal for stopping). Slow down, and make a final check over the left shoulder before pulling into the left to stop.*

Eye contact is particularly important on streets where there is not enough space for a following driver to overtake you. In these circumstances making eye contact is particularly important, and you should slow down gradually to make sure they are aware of what you are about to do.

4 Understand where to ride on roads being used

You should know the differences between the primary and secondary riding positions. Indicate where they are on the diagram below.

Can you name the advantages and disadvantages of each position?

Advantages   **Disadvantages**

Hint: *When cycling on the road, you should always position yourself where you can both see and be seen. You should also beware of cycling too close to the kerb, where drains, potholes and debris may obstruct you, and there is less room to take evasive action if necessary.*

The primary riding position, in the centre of the left-hand lane, will afford both you and other drivers the greatest visibility. It will also prevent drivers from attempting to overtake you where the road is too narrow, or where there is oncoming traffic. You should ride in the primary position on busy or narrow roads, and when you are riding at the speed of the other traffic.

The secondary riding position will allow you to be overtaken more easily, and is suitable for wide roads and/or low traffic. You should still remain at least half a metre from the kerb however, to avoid possible obstacles in the road and leave yourself room to manoeuvre if necessary.

5 Be aware of potential hazards

Think about the types of hazards that you might encounter when cycling. Name as many as you can.

Answers

Hint: *Good observation is important when cycling, and being aware of what hazards you may encounter will help you to prepare for them, and reduce the risks. You should be aware of other road users at all times, both in front of you and behind, and look behind you regularly to make sure other drivers are aware of your presence. Look out too for cars that might be preparing to turn across in front of you, or driveways from which vehicles might emerge into your path.*

*You should be aware, also, of pedestrians and others on the pavement ahead of you who might step into your path, and parked cars that might have their doors opened suddenly, as well as potential hazards such as drains and potholes on the road surfaces. **RULES 204–225** of the Highway Code (pages 54–69) highlight road users who require extra care.*

6 Make a U-turn

Practise making U-turns as tightly as you can.

What adjustment can you make to your bike to make keeping your balance easier?

Answer

Hint: *Like most manoeuvres, you'll be judged on your observation skills when U-turning. As you approach the point where you intend to turn, you must look back over your right shoulder to check for traffic behind you. If there's a safe gap both behind and in front, you can complete the turn. You should be able to make a U-turn within a normal two-lane road without leaving the carriageway.*

Balance is important when turning, as well as a low speed to prevent you from skidding. Selecting a low gear and keeping upright will help you to stay balanced.

7 Pass parked or slower-moving vehicles

Be aware of the potential hazards posed by parked or slow-moving vehicles. Name two things that might indicate that a parked car could pose a hazard to you.

Answers

1 ....

2 ....

Hint: *You should always observe behind you before pulling out to pass a parked vehicle. Ideally, try to cycle at least a car-door length away, to avoid the possibility of being hit by an opening door. If there is less room that this, due to narrow roads or oncoming traffic, slow down to an appropriate speed instead. Be wary, too, of cars that are about to pull away – people in the car, a running motor or a flashing indicator may be indicative of this.*

If there are a lot of parked cars in the road, it is safer to maintain your road position where you can be seen than to weave in and out between them. Remember to observe over your left shoulder before pulling back into the secondary position.

If you are cycling in queuing traffic, which side of the vehicles should you pass on?

Answer ....

Hint: *Just because a car is sitting in a queue, does not mean it won't pull over or make a left turn when you aren't expecting it. You should cycle to the right of queueing traffic wherever possible.*

8 Pass side roads

Name at least four things that you should look out for when approaching a side road.

Answers

1 .... 3 ....
2 .... 4 ....

Which is the correct riding position when passing a side road?

Answer ....

Hint: Hazards can come from all sides when passing a side road; you will need to look for vehicles that may be about to turn out of the road, vehicles on the opposite side of the road preparing to turn into it, and pedestrians who may be about to cross in front of you. To make yourself as visible as possible to drivers, and avoid the need to swerve around protruding vehicles, you should check over your shoulder for traffic behind and then move into the primary position. This will also prevent any vehicles following you from turning left across your path.

After passing the side road, you should make a final check over your left shoulder before moving back into your normal riding position. At a crossroads junction, remember that you must check for traffic emerging from the minor road on your right as well as on the left.

9 Understand how and when to signal intentions to other road users

Look at the arm signals below and indicate when you would use them. Practise using them as you ride.

Hint: *Signalling alerts other road users to your intentions, and should become a habit. It should always be combined with observation, particularly to your rear, though is not just of use to vehicles behind you – pedestrians and oncoming drivers may also warrant a signal.*

Make a clear signal with your arm extended as far from your body as possible; you may need to check that other drivers/riders have seen it. **RULE 103** *of The Highway Code (page 44) goes into more detail.*

10 Turn left into a minor road

Fill in the blanks and number the steps in the order that they should occur:

☐ Perform a final check over your _ _ _ _ shoulder for anyone trying to _ _ _ _ _ _ _ _ you.

☐ Check for _ _ _ _ _ _ _ in the minor road you are turning into, and _ _ _ _ _ _ _ _ _ _ who may be about to _ _ _ _ _ _ _ _ _ _ _ _ _.

☐ Heading towards the junction, look _ _ _ _ _ _ _ _ _ and move into the _ _ _ _ _ _ _ position.

☐ Complete the turn in the _ _ _ _ _ _ _ position.

☐ _ _ _ _ _ _ if necessary.

Hint: *Prior to turning, you should look behind you and move out into the primary position to prevent vehicles overtaking you and turning across your path (be aware that this does increase the possibility that someone might try to undertake you instead, so be sure to make one final check over your left shoulder before turning). Check for hazards in the road you are about to turn into, and watch out for any pedestrians crossing or preparing to cross the road at the head of the junction. If turning left at a crossroads, you should also check for traffic emerging on your right. Signal if necessary, perform a final check over your left shoulder, and make the turn in the primary position. Look at the diagram on page 73.*

11 & 12 Turn left into a major road; turn right into a major road

What additional steps do you need to take when turning left into a major road, rather than a minor one?

Answer ....

Hint: *When approaching a left turn into a major road, you should follow the usual steps of observing behind you, moving into the primary position (particularly important if you are going to need to stop, as it's when setting off that you'll be at your most unsteady and at risk from vehicles) and signalling your intentions if necessary. Additionally, you should decrease your speed and begin checking for traffic on the major road, particularly from your right. Stop or give way as appropriate, wait for a suitable gap in the traffic from your right and perform a final check over your left shoulder before turning.*

Which direction do you need to observe when turning right into a major road?

Answer ....

Hint: *When preparing to turn right into a major road, you must observe from all sides – behind you, traffic coming from both the left and the right and, if at a crossroads, traffic emerging from the minor road ahead of you. Signal as appropriate, and wait for a suitable gap in the traffic, but return both hands to the handlebars in time to brake or manoeuvre.*

TOP TIP

If the road ahead and behind you is clear it may not always be necessary to signal or stop at a Give Way sign after appropriate observation, but you should be able to explain your reasoning if questioned.

National Standard for Cycle Training – Level 2

13 Turn right from a major to minor road

After observing behind you, what are the two appropriate positions for you to move in to prior to making a right turn?

Answer ....

....

Hint: When turning right from a major to minor road, you will effectively have to turn across two different lanes of traffic. You should first observe behind you for a suitable gap in traffic, signal, and then, depending on how wide the road is and how confident you are, move into either the primary position or a position about an arm's length to the left of the centre line.

The primary position will prevent vehicles undertaking to your left, but if you are comfortable with traffic passing you on both sides, and the road is wide enough, you may choose to wait closer to the centre line. Whichever position you choose, you should make yourself visible and communicate with drivers going in both directions, and continue to signal if necessary.

When a suitable gap appears in the oncoming traffic, perform a final check over your right hand shoulder for any vehicles that may be attempting to overtake you before making the turn. Look at the diagram on page 75.

14 Demonstrate decision-making and understanding of safe riding strategy

Think about the times when you may need to display adaptability whilst cycling.

When would you *not* give way at a junction?

Answer ....

Can you think of an occasion when you may choose not to signal?

Answer ....

Hint: It is important that you not only understand the correct way to perform cycling manoeuvres, but are capable of adapting your behaviour to different circumstances. Make sure you know not just how to cycle safely, but why you are performing each action.

You should also have an understanding of the types of clothing you could wear to make yourself more visible (see page 28).

15 Demonstrate a basic understanding of *The Highway Code*

Read pages 26–93 and ensure that you understand the principles discussed.

Can you identify the following road signs and what they mean?

Hint: *Look at pages 60–65 if you aren't sure.*

National Standard for Cycle Training – Level 2

LEVEL 2 (OPTIONAL)

The following skills (16–18) are non-compulsory sections of the National Standard for Cycle Training, but it is recommended that all trainee riders ensure that they have an understanding of the theory and techniques outlined here.

16 Decide where cycle infrastructure can help a journey and demonstrate correct use

You should be able to decide whether or not to use cycle infrastructure, with regard to both safety and convenience, and explain your reasons. Refer to pages 32–37 for advice on cycle lanes.

17 Go straight on from minor road to minor road at a crossroads

You should be using similar techniques as you would for other manoeuvres – observation, signalling and positioning – with added awareness that you must be taking into account three different lanes of traffic that could pose a hazard to you. The Highway Code does not give clear guidance on who has priority if someone is also trying to emerge from the side road opposite you, so you must communicate effectively with them, and stop or give way to other traffic as appropriate.

18 Use mini-roundabouts and single-lane roundabouts

You should use the primary position on mini-roundabouts as it makes you more visible and prevents vehicles from overtaking you. Observe, signal if necessary, and stop at the Give Way line if it is necessary to give way to traffic already on the roundabout. Observe and signal again, if necessary, before exiting.

Be aware, also, that some drivers may drive over the central island of a mini-roundabout to pass you – maintain good observation and be ready to take evasive action if necessary.

Pages 78–81 give further advice for dealing with roundabouts.

1 Demonstrate knowledge of Level 2 (see pages 103–112)

2 Preparing for a journey

Explain how you would prepare for a cycling journey. Consider route planning, weather conditions, cycling at night and carrying luggage.

Answer ....

....

....

Hint: Planning your journey in advance, using a map or an electronic journey planner, will allow you to avoid difficult or dangerous junctions or road features, though you should still be capable of dealing with them if necessary. Check both the prevailing and forecast weather conditions before setting off, and plan accordingly – it may be necessary to carry additional clothing and accessories. Be aware that some conditions, such as snow or ice, will increase the risk of falls.

See RULE 60 (page 30) and page 31 for advice about riding at night. See pages 12–15 for information about suggested riding accessories.

3 Understanding advanced road positioning

As well as demonstrating confident use of the primary position in a variety of traffic environments, you should be able to show an understanding of when other positions in the road may be more appropriate, and why.

Why might you position yourself to the right of the lane when in a queue of vehicles, particularly when it contains HGVs?

Answer ....

Why should you not cycle too close when waiting behind or in front of a large vehicle such as an HGV?

Answer ....

Where should you wait at a junction where there are many cyclists present, and the cycle box is full?

Answer ....

Hints: Riders waiting in a traffic queue may position themselves to the right of the lane to be visible in the wing mirrors of queuing vehicles, particularly when behind HGVs. Cycling too closely to large vehicles means you won't be visible to the driver. A safe place to wait at a junction where there are many cyclists present in the box is in the primary position within the traffic queue or between lanes where they will be visible to other vehicles.

4 Passing queueing traffic

When encountering queueing traffic, you can either choose to pass it, on the left or the right (the right is generally preferable, as it makes you more visible to the majority of road users), or wait in the queue in the primary position.

When passing a queue, what should you be looking out for/prepared to stop for?

- Traffic in the queue that may _ _ _ _ _ _ _ _ _ _ _ _ _.
- _ _ _ _ _ _ _ _ _ _ _ _ _ _ _ _ _ _ _ _ in queueing cars so that _ _ _ _ _ _ _ _ _ can _ _ _ _ _ _.
- _ _ _ _ _ _ _ _ _ _ _ _ _ _ _ turning _ _ _ _ _ through a gap in the queue.
- Vehicles from the left _ _ _ _ _ _ _ _ _ _ of side roads or driveways _ _ _ _ _ _ _ _ _ _ _ _.

Hint: The ability to pass queueing traffic gives you an advantage in busy urban conditions, but must be done with care. It's your own choice whether to pass the traffic or wait in the queue – whether you are intending to turn left or right, or head straight on, may also inform your decision. Whichever option you choose, you should communicate with drivers in the queue to make them aware of your presence and what you are intending to do.

Be willing to wait if passing the queue will not help your journey, and be prepared to change your riding strategy if the queue changes (for example, if a vehicle starts to signal).

When passing a queue, you will need to be particularly vigilant for traffic in the queue that may turn across your path, nearside doors opening in queueing cars so that passengers can get out, oncoming traffic turning right through a gap in the queue, and vehicles from the left pulling out of from side roads or driveways into your path.

When should you never pass to the left of a long vehicle, bus or lorry?

Answer ....

Hint: You should never pass to the left of a long vehicle, bus or lorry at the head of a junction when approaching a left turn; you risk being caught in their blind spot.

5 Hazard perception and strategy to deal with hazards

Hazard perception can be divided into three parts:

- Where are you going? What are the potential hazards and manoeuvres ahead?
- What road users are around you? What obstructions might they cause you? Will you need to give them warning of your intentions?
- What do you need to do to complete the manoeuvre safely?

Look at the image below and identify the potential hazards. Explain how you would deal with each of them.

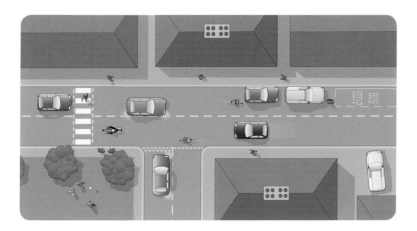

Hazards: **Resolutions:**

1 _____ ▶ _____
2 _____ ▶ _____
3 _____ ▶ _____
4 _____ ▶ _____
5 _____ ▶ _____
6 _____ ▶ _____
7 _____ ▶ _____
8 _____ ▶ _____

Hint: *Things to be on the lookout for include parked cars, pedestrians crossing behind parked cars, cars emerging from side roads and driveways, vehicles indicating that they are intending to make a turn, pedestrian crossings, playing children and many other variables. You may need to stop, signal, change your riding position, or even complete a manoeuvre as a pedestrian.*

6 Understanding driver blind spots, particularly for large vehicles

What is a blind spot?

Answer

Which vehicles pose a particular risk?

Answer

Where should you position yourself when waiting behind a large vehicle? On which side should you overtake them?

Answer

Hint: *A blind spot is any position in which you cannot be seen in either a driver's windscreen or one of their mirrors. They can be present on large vehicles such as HGVs and buses – if a driver can't see you, they can't take steps to avoid hitting you.*

Beware of stopping too close to the rear of a large vehicle – you should make sure you can see the driver's mirror, and try to make eye contact with the driver. If you choose to overtake, check over your shoulder beforehand and make sure to pass by on the right, never on the left. Try to make eye contact again once you are past, and never stop directly in front of a large vehicle – another blind spot.

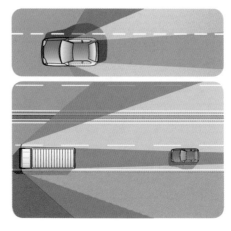

Blind spots are shown here for cars (top) and long vehicles (bottom). The red area indicates where a following vehicle cannot be seen by the driver.

7 Reacting to hazardous road surfaces

List as many potentially hazardous cycling surfaces as you can, and consider what action you would take to deal with each.

Hazards: **Actions:**

1 .... ▶ ....
2 .... ▶ ....
3 .... ▶ ....
4 .... ▶ ....
5 .... ▶ ....
6 .... ▶ ....
7 .... ▶ ....
8 .... ▶ ....

Hint: *Surfaces that are particularly hazardous to cyclists could include:*
- *Slippery surfaces, such as surfaces covered with water, oil, ice or wet leaves*
- *Roads with potholes*
- *Uneven surfaces, such as cobbled streets*
- *Metal surfaces (ie grids, manhole covers)*
- *Poorly maintained surfaces*
- *Tram lines*
- *Level crossings*
- *Speed humps and cushions*

You should be able to spot hazardous surfaces early, and decide on your course of action well in advance – either cycling over them with care, or avoiding them. If you encounter a slippery surface you should not brake or steer suddenly – reduce your speed gently and turn with care. When cycling over a hazardous surface you should steer as straight as possible, meeting the defect head on, and release the brakes. You can reduce discomfort by taking your weight off the saddle.

LEVEL 3 (OPTIONAL)

The following skills (8–17) are non-compulsory sections of the National Standard for Cycle Training, but it is recommended that all trainee riders ensure that they have an understanding of the theory and techniques outlined here.

8 How to use roundabouts

You should develop the skills learned in Level 2:18 (page 112), but now be able to confidently approach larger and multi-lane roundabouts as well. Observe how cars use the roundabouts, and behave in the same way as all other traffic – choose your lane, take up the primary position, and maintain this position throughout the manoeuvre, keeping in your lane. Identify the hazard spots at all points during the manoeuvre, and make eye contact with drivers who need to be aware of you.

Refer to the advice in the Highway Code on pages 78–81 for more details.

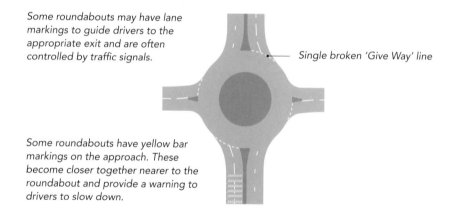

Some roundabouts may have lane markings to guide drivers to the appropriate exit and are often controlled by traffic signals.

Single broken 'Give Way' line

Some roundabouts have yellow bar markings on the approach. These become closer together nearer to the roundabout and provide a warning to drivers to slow down.

9 How to use junctions controlled by traffic lights

As a cyclist, you must obey traffic lights in the same way that all other traffic is expected to. See **RULE 071**, **RULE 109** and **RULES 175–178** (pages 70–71) for specifications.

When approaching traffic lights, you should take up the primary position in the centre of the lane appropriate for the manoeuvre you wish to carry out, and carry out observations and signalling as you would for an ordinary junction. If the lights are red, you should stop in the appropriate position, or move to the head of the queueing traffic if it is safe to do so (see Level 3:3 and Level 3:4).

10 How to use multi-lane roads

How you choose to use multi-lane roads will likely depend on how fast the traffic is moving, and if you are able to match its speed.

On urban roads, you may find it best to take the primary position in the lane that will facilitate the manoeuvre you wish to carry out, and match your speed to the traffic. Where speed limits are above 30mph, however, it is likely that you will find it safer to maintain the secondary position in the left-hand lane until nearing the point where lane selection is necessary, then move across making the appropriate observations and signals.

Where a journey is likely to require frequent changes of lane in fast-moving traffic, it may be worth considering alternative routes on quieter roads.

11 How to use both on- and off-road cycle infrastructure

Use of on- and off-road cycling facilities in the UK is not compulsory, but you should be aware of how to use them. Familiarise yourself with pages 32–41 of this book, particularly **RULE 061**, **RULE 062** and **RULE 063**.

You will be expected to demonstrate good observation, signalling and clear, confident positioning when using cycling infrastructure. Pay particular attention to use of advance stop lines (ASLs) and cycle boxes, and understand how they might help your journey. See also **RULE 178** (page 71).

National Standard for Cycle Training – Level 3

12 Dealing with vehicles that pull in and stop in front of you

Building on the techniques learned in Level 2:7 (page 106), you will be expected to demonstrate an ability to deal with vehicles that may stop in front of you such as buses, taxis and delivery vehicles. You should be able to identify vehicles that are likely to stop, decide whether or not to overtake – considering issues such as if you have time and space, particularly when passing long vehicles, and if it is likely that the vehicle may move off again quickly – and, if appropriate, overtake it safely.

For general advice from *The Highway Code* on overtaking, see RULES 162–169 (pages 48–50).

13 Sharing the road with other cyclists

You should be able to demonstrate effective communication and positioning techniques when cycling in areas where other cyclists are present. You should use frequent observation over your left shoulder to ensure that you are aware of other cyclists passing inside you, and use the techniques learned in Level 2:7 (page 106) to overtake when necessary.

When overtaking a cyclist using a cycle lane, you should treat this as if you are changing lanes, combining the techniques from Level 2:7 with those from Level 3:10 (page 119). Be aware that drivers may not be expecting you to leave the cycle lane and make sure that you are communicating your intentions effectively. Read also *The Highway Code* RULES 211–213 (page 58) for drivers with regard to cyclists.

When using the primary position at junctions where other cyclists are present, be aware of other cyclists using the secondary position. If the junction has an ASL/cycle box that is already congested with other cyclists, take an appropriate position either within the traffic queue, in the filter lane, or on the line between lanes.

14 Cycling on roads with a speed limit above 30mph

On roads with higher speed limits, drivers have less time to react and stopping distances are greater. You must demonstrate that you allow more time before manoeuvring, and that you can judge the speed and distance of vehicles around you. You may find it necessary to take the secondary position more often.

 For general advice on speed limits, see page 51.

15 Cycling in bus lanes

You will be expected to understand bus lane signage (see pages 38–39) and understand how it affects your journey. Take the centre of the lane unless it is necessary to let vehicles pass, and be able to decide for yourself when you should let a vehicle pass you.

Take particular care when bus lanes cross side roads, and also remain on the alert for illegal use of bus lanes by unauthorised vehicles, who may not be looking out for cyclists.

16 Cycling in pairs or groups

You should practise cycling in pairs or groups, being careful not to cycle so close to each other that you cannot react to sudden changes in speed or direction from the cyclist in front. You are responsible for your own positioning, signalling and communication, but can help each other by calling out any hazards such as potholes or other vehicles. If riding two abreast, be aware that this may aggravate some other road users and you must be ready to move back into single file if the situation calls for it.

17 Locking a bike securely

You should demonstrate an understanding of the safer places to lock your bike, and the preferred type of cycle stand to use. Know the pros and cons of different types of lock and which parts of your bicycle to lock to the stand – be aware, also, of the different parts of a bicycle that can be removed by thieves!

For advice on cycle security, see pages 52–53.

Further Information

Where to ride

Though completion of the Bikeability course should leave you a confident cyclist on most roads, it is worth making sure you are aware of off-road and safer on-road routes, and can take them into account when planning your journey.

National Cycle Network

Covering more than 14,000 miles and stretching across the length and breadth of the UK, the National Cycling Network is a series of on-road cycling routes and traffic-free paths designed to allow cyclists, pedestrians and other vulnerable road users to make their journeys in safe conditions, away from busy, traffic-filled roads.

It is also host to one of Britain's biggest collections of public art, with local artists commissioned to design sculptures, benches, water fountains, viewing points and bridges to enhance its routes. And if you've decided to take up cycling for environmental reasons, rest assured: the network is committed to conserving wildlife and habitats and promoting biodiversity on its traffic-free routes.

Routes on the National Cycle Network connect most of the major towns and cities in Britain, and are split into national and regional cycling routes. National routes are indicated by a number on a red patch, and regional routes by a number on a blue patch – look out for them on blue road signs marked with a cycle symbol.

The National Cycle Network is managed by Sustrans, a charity promoting sustainable transport, though many of the routes themselves are on land owned and maintained by local authorities, highways agencies and other landowners. To find out more about the many routes visit sustrans.org.uk.

Primary route-direction sign, in advance of a junction, indicating a route for cyclists

Non-primary route-direction sign, in advance of a junction, indicating a route for cyclists

Number of a national cycle route

Number of a regional cycle route

Sign showing the direction and distances (in miles) to destinations along a named cycle route forming part of the National Cycle Network

Sign indicating two different cycle routes leading from a junction ahead

This sign informs you that you are following a national cycle route, with the number shown

Map-type signs may indicate the route through a junction. In this example, the sign shows the route across an entry slip road. A sign may be used to direct cyclists to a signal-controlled crossing

Direction of a national cycle route

Signs indicating the direction to a parking place for pedal cycles

Planning a journey

Cycle-specific journey planners such as cyclestreets.net and bikehub.co.uk offer route planning for cyclists, often with a choice of routes including 'quietest' or 'fastest'. They also include routes via cycle paths. If using a phone or other device to navigate, however, you should take care not to allow it to distract you from observing your surroundings, and use your common sense – if your own eyes or knowledge tells you that a suggested route is inappropriate, you should choose an alternative rather than blindly following directions.

In London, you can plan your journey using the Transport for London (TfL) journey planner (tfl.gov.uk), which offers both direct cycling routes (with a choice of easy, moderate or fastest, depending on your requirements) and routes that will allow you to take advantage of the cycle hire scheme.

Off-road Cycling

Off-road cycling can encompass anything from cycling along a cycle path to downhill mountain biking, and everything in between. It can be an excellent option for family cycling, given that, by its nature, it avoids road traffic.

The main types of off-road cycling

- **Cycle paths** – quite simply any designated path for cyclists. These are usually signposted and are frequently in towns, cities or villages.
- **Cycling Centres** – these are usually found in forestry and country parks and are often family-focused but not exclusively so. They frequently combine well-signposted, flat, off-road cycling routes for families with a variety of other, often more challenging, routes suitable for experienced riders.
- **Mountain bike-trail centres** – Similar to family cycling centres in location but more focused on purpose-built technical mountain-biking routes. These usually include different routes to allow for a variety of experience levels.
- **Canal towpaths** – flat and usually easy to get to, these are often a great way to travel between towns via a scenic and traffic-free route.
- **Parks** – not all parks allow cycling, but in those that do, it's best to assume slow speeds and ride with other park users in mind.
- **Bridleways and byways** – the only real way to get out into the countryside at large. Ordnance Survey maps or a guidebook or routemap are advisable.

In the majority of off-road cycling environments – apart from cycling centres and mountain-bike trail centres – a rider will be sharing their route with those on foot and, potentially, also horse riders. This shared-use environment brings with it a responsibility to be respectful and tolerant, for all concerned.

Off-road code of conduct

- **Only ride where it is legal to do so.** It is forbidden to cycle on public footpaths unless they are clearly marked as shared-use paths, usually with a blue sign. The only non-designated 'rights of way' open to cyclists are bridleways and unsurfaced tracks, known as byways, which are open to all traffic.*
- **On designated cycle ways shared with pedestrians, always keep to the side intended for cyclists.** The other side remains a footpath and therefore out of bounds. Care should be taken when passing pedestrians, particularly children, elderly people or disabled people, or those with dogs. Allow plenty of space.
- **Canal towpaths:** these are not rights of way, but rather permissive paths where cycling is allowed by the Canal & River Trust (www.canalrivertrust.org.uk), but only within their guidelines. Remember that towpaths can sometimes be closed for maintenance and access paths can be steep and slippery. Bikes are best pushed by hand rather than ridden under low bridges and by locks.
- **Always yield to walkers and horses**, giving adequate but polite warning of approach. A cheery 'hello' or 'excuse me' can be a gentle way of forewarning other trail users.
- **Take care at trail junctions** and any road crossing points and always be aware of other trail users.
- **Don't expect to cycle at high speeds.**
- **Keep to the main trail** to avoid any unnecessary erosion to surrounding areas and to prevent skidding, especially if it is wet.
- **Always be aware of the likely presence of dogs, livestock and wild animals.**
- **Remember the Countryside Code** (www.gov.uk/government/publications/the-countryside-code).

The presence of bikes in popular hillwalking areas, even on legitimate rights of way, can be a contentious one, sometimes leading to conflict between cyclists and walkers. The best approach is to be polite and respectful at all times.

*The Scottish Outdoor Access Code (www.outdooraccess-scotland.com) gives the right of access over all land and inland water to walkers, horse riders and cyclists for recreation or education – providing they act in a responsible fashion.

The Road User and the Law

The road-traffic laws below are found in abbreviated form between pages 26 and 93. For the precise wording of the law, acts and regulations since 1988 can be read at www.legislation.gov.uk. Prior to 1988, in print from The Stationery Office.

CUR	Road Vehicles (Construction & Use) Regulations 1986
FTWO	Functions of Traffic Wardens Order 1970
HA	Highway Act 1835 or 1980 (as indicated)
MT(E&W)R	Motorways Traffic (England & Wales) Regulations 1982
MT(E&W)(A)R	Motorways Traffic (England & Wales) Amended Regulations
MT(S)R	Motorways Traffic (Scotland) Regulations 1995
MV(VSL)(E&W)	Motor Vehicles (Variation of Speed Limits) (England & Wales) 2014
PCUR	Pedal Cycles (Construction & Use) Regulations 1983
RTRA	Road Traffic Regulation Act 1984
R(S)A	Roads (Scotland) Act 1984
PRA	Police Reform Act 2002
RSA	Road Safety Act 2006
RTA	Road Traffic Act 1984, 1988 and 1991
RVLR	Road Vehicles Lighting Regulations 1989
TMA	Traffic Management Act 2004
TSRGD	Traffic Signs Regulations & General Directions 2002
ZPPPCRGD	Zebra, Pelican and Puffin Pedestrian Crossings Regulations and General Directions 1997

Most apply on all roads throughout Great Britain, although there are exceptions. The definition of a road in England and Wales is 'any highway and any other road to which the public has access and includes bridges over which a road passes' (RTA 1988 sect 192(1)). In Scotland, a similar definition includes any way over which the public have a right of passage (R(S)A 1984 sect 151(1)). References to 'road' therefore generally include footpaths, bridleways and cycle tracks, and many roadways and driveways on private land (including many car parks). There may be additional rules for particular paths or ways. Some serious driving offences, including drink-driving offences, also apply to all public places.

The Highway Code and the law

'MUST/MUST NOT' rules in the Code are legal requirements, and if disobeyed are a criminal offences. Cyclists may be fined (maximum fines: dangerous cycling – £1,000; careless cycling – £1,000; cycling on pavement – £500). Drivers may be given penalty points or be disqualified. In serious cases, prison is an option.

Although failure to comply with the other rules will not, in itself, cause a person to be prosecuted, *The Highway Code* may be used in evidence in any court proceedings under the Traffic Acts to establish liability. This includes rules that use advisory wording such as 'should/should not' or 'do/do not'.

Index

Newport Library and Information Service

Useful Contacts

CYCLING ORGANISATIONS

Bicycle Association,
bicycleassociation.org.uk
An industry organisation,
founded in 1890, which represents
the British bicycle industry.

Bikeability
bikeability.org.uk
The government-recognised
training programme for cyclists.

British Cycling
britishcycling.org.uk
The governing body for cycling
in Great Britain, and home to
the GB cycling team, as well
as information for all riders.

CTC
ctc.org.uk
The UK's national cycling charity
aims to inspire and help people
to cycle.

Cyclenation
cyclenation.org.uk
Helping local groups to campaign
and to represent them at the
national and international level.

**International Mountain Biking
Association UK**
www.IMBA.org.uk
Offers detailed information on
mountain-bike policy and practice.

Sustrans
sustrans.org.uk
A national charity campaigning
for more journeys to be made by
bike. They created the National
Cycle Network.

SAFETY AND FIRST AID

British Red Cross
www.redcross.org.uk
Offers first-aid advice and training
across the UK.

Road Safety GB
www.roadsafetygb.org.uk
National road-safety organisation.

**The Royal Society for the
Prevention of Accidents**
www.rospa.com
Safety and injury prevention advice,
including road safety.

Think!
think.direct.gov.uk
Road-safety advice for all
road users.

St John Ambulance
www.sja.org.uk
UK-wide charity teaching first
-aid skills.

St Andrew's First Aid
www.firstaid.org.uk
First-aid charity in Scotland
offering training and advice.